First published in Great Britain in 1997 by
TRIUMPH HOUSE
1 - 2 Wainman Road, Woodston,
Peterborough, PE2 7BU

HB ISBN 1 86161 146 3
SB ISBN 1 86161 141 2

Foreword

Many people use poetry as a way of communication to share their emotions with loved ones and pass on their thoughts to friends.

The poets included in this anthology have joined hands to bring their emotions together and they delve deep into creativity to write about the things that we hold close to our hearts.

Together the writers have created a wonderful collection of inspirational stories and messages that offer a wealth of information and insight into the Christian faith.

Chris Walton
Editor

CONTENTS

ONE VOYAGE OF DISCOVERY

Christmas - one voyage of discovery
Birthing the future, bring forth the young
Ideas in concept, created and sung
Each relative to what we make
But hearing hope for Goodness sake
Instead of loads of mindless rush
Of hasty preparations and fuss
Remember that's what the Child represents
Here and now in the present.

Colette Cullen

FOUR SEASONS

Spring, summer, autumn, winter,
Oh how the seasons fly,
You've scarce got over winter,
Till you find you're in July.
But each season has its beauty
And not just spring alone,
So enjoy each season as it comes
And don't just sit and moan.
For the cold wind in the winter
Has its own part to play,
And if the rain should cease to fall,
We'd have good cause to pray.
For the good Lord knows what is best for us
And yet we still complain,
While some folk in a desert live,
That we get too much rain.
So just give thanks for every day
Whatever it may bring.

Robert Calwell

THE GREATEST LOVE OF ALL

'Love' is such a little word
but there's a plentiful supply
of different meanings and of feelings
that none of us can deny.

That special love of children,
full of trust, there is no doubt.
Their love's so pure and innocent,
it radiates from inside, out.

A parent's love is deeper,
there is no way to measure
the way it protects and embraces
and brings children so much pleasure.

There is a special fondness
that only friendship shares.
A warm and comforting feeling,
to know that someone cares.

The ardour of that precious love
between a husband and a wife,
that caring, sharing, needed love
that will last you all your life.

But now I've found another love,
a greater love I can't recall,
for God's love must surely be
the greatest love of all.

Karen Husband

YOUTH BEWARE
(From concern about temptations facing young people.)

Party to lying, cheating, swearing.
Ungodly thoughts coming from within.
Separating man from God and filling like a dustbin,
That part of us designed to hold purity and truth.
Peer group pressure enticing the young to follow suit,
A quick fag behind the bike sheds -
No-one will know!
But the ache is there inside - that pain caused by guilt,
Knowing that the dustbin now holds a little more.
Visual temptations via papers and TV,
Just one trip on drugs is all it need be.
'Get real', you say, 'we're fine, we know what we're doing',
But do you, in reality know where you're going -
With no feeling of purpose, no sense of fulfilment -
To a life without God!
These things that attract in the time known as youth
Just lead further away from the truth.
There is only one answer to youth's strong desires,
One safe way that won't leave you playing with fires.
That will soothe those deep longings,
To feel loved and accepted,
And heal those guilt feelings that only you know.
Turn now to Jesus and ask His forgiveness
For all those things that can drag you so low.
He'll empty the garbage from that inner dustbin
And fill up the space with what He designed,
He'll show you life's purpose and give you fulfilment,
Placing your hands in God's.

Diane Mackintosh

THE WORLD AT ONE

The World At One how wonderful it would be -
If this were true in its intensity,
No farther from the truth has this become,
For never was it less - The World At One.

With wars and greed and torment the world o'er,
Oppressions lack of trust and so much more,
Famines and pestilence still have their run,
How far removed from fact
The World At One.

There's strikes and disputes with the workers here,
And trouble in the Nations over there,
No peace, just only fear of things to come.
It seems 'twill never be
The World At One.

Men do their best to put this old world right,
But God says 'By My Spirit' not by might -
Obey my word - repent, accept my son,
Only when men's hearts are changed, will it be,
The World At One.

Phyllis Pearce

MY FRIEND MARY

A smiling face with a cheeky grin
Yet no-one knew what lay within.
Years of pain, jibes and frustration
Long dark years, occasionally elation.

Days of hope, spirits raised again
Hopes of walking straight, not lame.
Yet one look at her mother's face
Said it all - not in this case.

'Why me?' frequently crossed her mind
As she limped along far behind.
What will become of me in the years to come?
When my legs seize up and my strength is gone.

In the background is a White Knight
Who will see that she is alright.
Her brain is sharp and sometimes her tongue
But she is loved and respected by everyone.

Brenda Bartlett

ABANDONED!

I found a bundle at my door,
One sunny Sunday morn,
Lying still and silent there,
Abandoned and forlorn.

Carefully I picked it up
And carried it inside,
Tenderly cradled in my arms,
To my husband sadly sighed ...

'Who could have done this and oh why
Did they not leave a note?
Makes me feel so sad', I said,
As a lump came to my throat.

It was perfect, pink and plump,
And so beautifully formed,
I washed it very carefully,
And made sure 'twas gently warmed.

So to whom it may concern,
This message comes, oh my,
Thank you for the rhubarb,
It made a super pie!

G Whitear

I LOVE YOU BECAUSE

I love you because
you accept me as I am,
I love you because,
when I say I can't, you say I can.
I love you for your gentleness,
in dealing Lord with me,
for areas where I was blind before
and now you help me see.
I love you for adopting me
and calling me your own,
I love you for your Fatherhood
and because of that I've grown.
I love you for your faithfulness,
Lord you've never let me down,
in all the times, good and bad, you've always been around.
I love you so much Lord,
my words really fail to express,
to a heart that once was empty
you've brought lifelong happiness.

Yvonne Neal

WELLS CATHEDRAL

I step inside and look with awe
and think of others years ago
who stood within this place right here
to pray or wed or shed a tear.

The architect who planned this place
for spiritual need
exceeded tenfold in his quest
the faithful for to feed.

The staircase, wonder, to behold
it is a man made dream
the choice to follow with the mass
or seek eternal peace.

A time capsule preserved in stone
for those of weary mind
a sanctuary for us all
in Wells Cathedral find.

Cyclops

TILL THEN

It isn't always easy to face another day,
Knowing that your loved one isn't there to share your way,
It's not so much the mountains, you've learned to cope with those,
It's the little, sudden, simple things, to which your mind can't close.
The bitter-sweet remembrance of a dear familiar tune
That perhaps has been a favourite, and you feel 'Lord, it's too soon'.
And often, even harder, is the need to talk once more,
To tell your loved one bits of news when you walk in the door.
How wonderful to realise - our dear Lord understands,
He's there beside us all the while, with loving outstretched hands.
He doesn't ask us to forget - He gave us memories
To look back with a grateful heart to precious things like these.
He only asks that we commit our pains, our heartaches, tears
Into His loving, patient care - He longs to calm our fears.
And as we come into the place that He would have us be,
He takes us just the way we are - He so loves you and me.
And one day when this life is done, and we all meet again,
There'll only be great joy and peace - no parting and no pain.
'Till then we know He'll see us through - He'll give us of His grace.
So praise the Lord, let's soldier on - until we see His face.

Carol A Howard

THE HOMECOMING

As I walked down the lane tired, hurt and hungry
My mind returned to the year before
I had left home full of hope, confidence and my
own self importance.
I had left my parents hurting and grieving, I'll never
know how much.

I felt I knew best, I knew all the answers,
My parents were old fashioned, they did not understand,
I was going to live a little
So I was going to the big city.

I was soon to realise I did not know all the answers
And my parents may be old fashioned but they knew best.
My steps dragged and I cuddled my little bundle closely,
My little baby girl, I was a parent now and
Understood a little more.

And then I found new strength, from where? I knew not where,
But it came and I started to quicken my pace
Holding even closer my precious bundle,
I wanted to walk that lane as fast as I could.

Because I knew when I reached home
The door would be open
The welcome would be warm
And I would be loved as though I'd never left,
My parents had always loved me with an unconditional love
And I was going home.

Olive Birkett

THE PROMISE

When the storm clouds have gathered,
And the thunder gives voice to a roar,
When everything seems set against you,
And you think there just couldn't be more.
Just remember God's promise to Noah.
On His words, you too can rely.
The darkness will not last forever,
Look for the rainbow God set in the sky.

Rita Scott

REMEMBER

You can remember what happened
    A long time ago,
But what happened yesterday?
    The answer is 'no'.

One's daily routine is
    A regular thing.
You can answer the doorbell
    If it should ring.

But you go upstairs for something,
    And you can't remember what.
Come down, and you'll remember,
    As likely as not.

Ask the Good Lord to help you,
    And try not to fall.
We're all getting older,
    It's the same for us all.

Elizabeth Bovill

THE DEAR PRESENCE OF CHRIST

Lord, my need is so great,
teach me to listen, and wait
on you every passing day:
until I know
the way to go;
please help me be faithful and pray.

Lord, the darkness is near,
but you save me from all fear:
I am in you, safely kept
from the night -
surrounded with light:
secure whenever I've slept.

Lord, my head feels so weary,
please, dear Lord, draw near me:
order my thinking and feeling.
Trusting in you,
help me pull through;
in my heart I am constantly kneeling.

Lord, life can be lonesome at times,
the devil accuses with crimes;
but your Word is sincere and true -
it never fails,
when everything ails
it reminds us of all that you do.

For you bring good news to the earth:
your promises lighten the dearth
that can surround us each day,
when evil's near
we hold onto the dear
presence of Christ in the way ...

Richard D Reddell

ABUNDANT LIFE!

There came a time many years ago,
When I came to know
The Lord Jesus Christ
Had died for me.

God spoke to my heart for many days,
In lots of ways,
Before light dawned
And life was changed.

He called for my response,
Not just once,
But time and time again
Till my heart said 'yes'.

Joy filled my soul,
Now I was whole,
Jesus was mine
And I was His.

Life more abundant started that day,
Now come what may,
God is within,
I've accepted Him.

He is my Father,
I am His child,
Jesus my Saviour
Spirit my guide.

Elsie Heys

WHAT A STATE WE'RE IN

Never thought I would say 'I remember when'.
Where is England's fire and spark.
Why do some still live in a cardboard box.
A shop doorway, a bench in a park?

Some politicians offer solutions to problems.
At this they say they're adept.
It may work out theoretically on paper.
Not practical though, just inept.

Promises made for a wonderful future.
In winter, summer, any season.
Then somehow the whole thing flies through the window.
Cancelled for no special reason.

Uneasiness seems to pervade the air.
Have some of the very young gone barmy.
No second thought before wielding a knife?
Joining willingly the Evil One's army.

There must be a way to serenity and peace.
Where ever we are we can pray.
The need is urgent to walk tall, speak freely.
To welcome the dawn of each day.

Violette Edwards

THE END AND THE BEGINNING

When evil has o'ertaken earthly days,
Not even God remembered in the haze,
Shall start the final fight for earthly reign
And Truth shall be a sword which leaves men slain.
Twisted torture; deathly din; battle rage,
Unsurpassed by cruelty in any age,
Satan, and all his demons crushed, o'erpast.
A peaceful reign, a thousand years to last.

And in eternal hope and silent sleep,
The dead, o'er which your heavenly angels keep,
Will, while the earth's last leaders fall
Shall rise from slumber by the trumpet call
To free their souls for ever from the sod
And see their heart's desire, The Lamb of God.
For evermore, yet infinite the days,
Lay at your feet and sing eternal praise.

J G Ryder

MEMORIES

All is quiet, all is still,
Yet in times gone by all was busy as a mill,
In yuletide seasons children played,
Their home-made gifts proudly displayed.

In spring the tulips grew by the dozens,
Preceded by the daffodils their cousins,
Children ran and laughed and squealed,
Up and down the overgrown field.

Summertime brought umpteen joys,
Trees were used as favourite toys,
Little voices could be heard dancing, giggling
            having fun,
Under the awesome shining sun.

Bonfire night was better still,
Compost heap piled up like a hill,
Flames curving up so high,
Further and further into the sky.

Yet now all are gone so far,
I feel alone 'til I hear shouts of 'Grandpa',
The past is relived in the present,
The moon shines down in a crescent!

Maria McGrath

PROVISION

I gave away a pound or two,
To someone with a lack,
But, in a day or two, behold,
I found it coming back.
Then, when a need I met, but with a cost,
(if truth be told,)
Oh what delight, to find the sum
Returning doublefold.
If I could have, both wealth enough,
And wisdom's inner eye,
To see where lies the greatest need
Some void to satisfy,
For Lord, it is your earnest plan
For those who gain success,
(From out of your vast treasury store)
To succour those with less.
I guess it takes a special trust,
With gifted wealth, or fame,
To keep the heart from planting
tempting roots of greedy gain.
So, as I trust for my supply,
Whatever, great or small,
Just make me faithful, and content
with anything at all.

M K Malloy

OUTSIDE TO WITHIN

Don't feel scared by your shortfalls.
Jesus understands.
He won't forget if you're struggling
Your name is written on His hands.
He paid the price and died for you
because you mean so much to Him.
He has brought you through the curtain
from the outside to within.

Don't be hurt when life's pitfalls
Beat you black and blue.
Jesus stood where you're standing
He knows what you're going through.
So look up, let Him lift you
from the pain and hurt you're in.
His love will fill and heal you
from the outside to within.

Family! We're together
One with the Father through the Son.
With Jesus Christ Lord and Saviour
The victory has been won.
United through His bloodshed.
Ultimate payment for all sin.
He's brought us through the curtain
from the outside to within.

Jacqueline Mary Wilkinson

GRACE

God is great there is no doubt.
Yes he's great, shout it out.
Praise him, the very stones will.
He made it all, from the valley
to the highest hill.

God the maker of the human race.
Why did he bother you may ask?
Why did he put man in control?
Has he gone away and left us on
our own.

The problem is my dear friend,
He gave man his own free will.
He let man choose which way to go,
He gave his law to use to obey.
Man thought he could do it his own way.

All the sorrow and the pain,
began in the garden, when Satan
said 'You will not die, just eat
the fruit and to my way, and sin,
sin, sin.
Now that I am in control man
doesn't know the trouble he's in.'

So God sent Jesus to give man
another chance.
He died for the whole human race.
It's all to do with grace, grace,
grace.

Kevin J Herbert

BABY BLUES

God, are you there?
Have you really reached out to me -
>have you let me go?
>Christians shouldn't be depressed!
>Pull yourself together!
My children - how can I bring them up?
Am I feeding the baby properly?
I can't even cook.
Am I doing enough for the toddler?
I can't read to her, let alone play.
>You've got such a lovely family,
>You ought to be grateful!
>There are plenty worse off than you!
I'm guilty, what have I done?
Are you punishing me God?
Where do I find springs of living water?
I'm drowning in wells of tears.
>You ought to get out more, mix with people!
>You need a job - to take you out of yourself!
Who can understand my burden, who knows my thoughts?
Help me someone - can anyone?
Please tell me what I need to hear!

Why don't you tell me to fix my eyes on Jesus?

Isabel Bekircan

CAST OFF THE SHACKLES

The burden of this life is heavy,
Stone filled hearts and minds of clay,
Despair crouches in the corner
Like an almighty beast of prey.

Within the breast turmoil settles,
Tortured souls writhe, piercing eyes
survey this world of senseless evil
that man imparts upon the skies.

Splendid memories of Manhood
come to earth in infant form,
He touches this dark world with pity,
Hope, compassion, love are born.

Majestic Son of God, your glory
fills the sinner's soul with peace,
Why then, why do we ignore you,
Will our struggles never cease?

On a wooden cross at Calvary,
You shed Your precious blood that day,
Giving life and your Salvation
to all Mankind on Judgement day.

Come into our lives Sweet Jesus,
Fill our hopeless empty hearts,
That we may at Life's departure,
Know all thy blessed love imparts.

Off the shackles of dread mourning,
Clothe our souls in splendour bright,
Christ is Risen, oh happy dawning,
Onward into Glory Bright.

Susan Edwards

LIFE'S MYSTERY

Life will remain when we have gone
to a place unknown, in time beyond
Man's understanding of this life,
of malice, anger, war and strife.

What is there which we don't see
because of mere mortality?
A universe of mystery,
unfolding slowly by degree.

A human life that marvels sights
reflected in a clear still night,
of starlit wonders, there amassed,
in galaxy's expanse, so vast.

Gazing into void above
one wonders if it could, or would,
have been the same as we each know,
without our Lord's creative glow.

Stephen R Garner

THE VINE

Gather your strength from the vine.
the vine is the Father divine.
He sends out his branches so fine,
With grapes that are ready for wine.
We all drink from the one loving cup,
With lips that are eager to sup.
For love of His name,
We will not find fame,
As the flame of His love burns us up.

M Madej

FOR BABY

This world born into, isn't much,
With wars and famine, drought and such,
but if you'll try, don't spill your tears
for this, and as you grow in years,
you'll come to know that love is found
like raindrops nourishing the ground,
all fears and pain tho' trampled there,
are banished by it - so is care -
so face Life's run and dry your eyes,
Life can be fun, it's no surprise,
this world we give you *has* a dove -
in peace and hope ... we give you love.

Enid Vaughan

CALLED AWAY

I sit beside him, waiting for a sign,
A twitch, or any move that says 'I'm here'.
The stillness is unbroken. In fear
I tremble. With his lifeless hand in mine
I yearn to draw him back across the line
Dividing us. Can no one urge him near
To me? He was pulsating life - so dear!
O Lord!, I'm begging at your throne divine
For life - his life - O Father hear my plea!
If no tomorrow is, for him, Your will,
Grant in Your mercy strength enough for me
To live each day as he would wish - until
That Day when - face to face - we'll be
Hearing Your benediction - 'Peace - be still!'

Joan Perry

DARKNESS AND LIGHT

There was darkness
now it's bright,
Now Jesus I can
see the light.
I was all for myself
and money,
Now it is just as sweet as honey.
I was always giving cheek,
Jesus I thank you
for letting me seek.
Now I'm not for myself
any more.
Thank you for opening
a new door.

C Johnston

THE BIRDS IN THE GARDEN

The birds in the garden sit in the tree,
Paired in love,
I wish they were me.

Free to roam, free to search,
Seeing life from that eternal perch.
Angelic innocence,
Glory is theirs,
Joyously sharing God's worldly cares.

They knew His son, they now know me,
The difference must be marked,
Oh God help me!

Paul Gainsford Bailey

FROM TREE TO TOMB

Alone,
I sit
engulfed in uncertainty,
my life a void.
'Where are you God?'
a cry from my soul
echoes in the gloom.
Silence.
I bow in submission
to the darkness,
to the pain.
Tears betray my inner torment.
And yet
in my despair
I see a flicker of light,
A hand
once crucified stretches,
pleads for my grasp.
The stone rolls away from my tomb of despair.
I stand tall
erect,
bereft of hopelessness,
clothed in light and love.
From death to life
I have made the journey.
From tree to tomb
I have come,
to share His life
no longer alone.

Andrew Daniel Lawler

THE PAIN OF LIFE
(From counselling experience not *personal experience)*

I am hurting deep inside my heart,
The memories I carry they tear me apart,
My childhood went so quickly, of it I feel robbed,
Many times I have sat alone, I have cried and I have sobbed.

My father with his sexual desire, he's hurt me deep within,
Nobody sees the hurt I feel because of demanding sin.
The mental, physical me, with its anger cannot cope at all,
Jesus will you take the pain, as on you I do call.

I know for me you bled and died, on the cross at Calvary,
To set me free, from such pain, to bring me liberty,
My unforgiveness, my memories, they have been with me for years.
Help me overcome the pain and trauma, bringing me much fear.

I release myself to you O Lord, to do with me now whatever,
I welcome you, your love, your power, to bring healing and to sever.
Bring your peace into this situation Lord, give me peace of mind.
Be my Saviour, Lord and Friend, please accept me as you find.

D Beckingham

RIDE THE WINDS

I will ride the winds right up to heaven.
Knowing God is waiting for me there.
I will land on top of his bright rainbow.
Drink deeply of the pure clean evening air.
Listen to the Angel choirs all singing.
While their golden harps they softly play.
Wonderful sweet music which keeps ringing.
While I thank my God for my today.

Amen.

Barbara Goode

FIFTY

A milestone?
A peak?
A watershed?

An age when
The rear-vision mirror holds more of life
Than the wide-horizoned windscreen.

When the old longings to be
Desired, loved, accepted
Still remain (with their pain)
Behind a facade of experience and maturity.

An age when
Your children offer answers
To your unsolved problems
While you ponder on the meaning of life.

A time for
Regret, reflection, renewal.
Serenity replacing striving.
Being outclassing doing.
Loving outweighing being loved.

A time when
Hope reasserted and
Confidence restored bring the
Realisation of unfulfilled dreams
In a future yet to be revealed!

Margaret Bardsley

THE NAME

When God's creation was still new
and all was fresh as morning dew,
when He'd made the sun, stars and moon,
a wet morning and a sunny afternoon,
He wanted to give a name to everything
from owls that hoot to birds that sing.
After a week, only one thing remained
that was still waiting to be named.
Because He wanted to get the name right,
God meditated all day and into the night.

It was a gentle thing, with love overflowing
and seemed to have its own way of knowing
good from bad and right from wrong
and in its heart there was always a song.
It possessed courage, strong and unbending,
a will of iron, and a knack for attending
to any task God set it, with determination,
would even face danger, and starvation
to protect those that God placed in its care,
it had love to share and love to spare.

It had a gift of kissing away pain
and making dull days seem sunny again.
Even when its own heart was breaking
it carried on with its home-making.
It was full of cuddles and warm embraces
that turned frowns into smiling faces.
'I have it,' God smiled, 'more than any other,
the name that suits it best is ... Mother.'

Lucinda Hearne

DEVELOPING

The film's in the camera, the subject sits waiting,
To see the result he's anticipating.
The photographer focuses, holds it quite steady,
Taking the photo when his sitter is ready.
But still the result of the picture's not known,
The film must be processed, the developing done.

Into the darkroom the film must be taken,
And special equipment is used in the making,
To give correct vision just one special light,
The shadows outside just wouldn't be right.
The film would be spoiled if not handled so,
For the master technician the right method will know.

The correct temperature must be kept all the while,
If the subject's to see the result of his smile.
The timing is crucial, too short or too long,
And the picture will be developed all wrong.
In all the processes, the skill of the trade,
Must be used to the best, good results to be made.

And, so it is, too, in the Christian way,
The image is captured on Salvation day,
But the process of life must be rightly enveloped
By time and by heat and by light so developed,
That the image of Christ which was given us then,
Will develop within us, and make us like Him.

Jenny Dukes

TIME - TODAY

Narrow lanes, roaming bends,
Ups and downs, never ends.
Flowing streams, pleasing dreams,
All of this is in my past.
I have found joy.
The straight and narrow.
He will be the light under my feet
And alas no more sorrow.

K G Shone

SEE THINGS MORE MY WAY

I wanted to argue that it really wasn't practical
That You couldn't expect me to aspire to the heights
        that you had reached,
Surely all that matters are my good intentions,
Just as long as one the whole I agree with what
        You preached.

I wanted to show you that now things are different,
That life isn't as simple as it once used to be,
Today, being narrow-minded really isn't acceptable,
I wanted to show you just how hard things are for me.

But at every persuasive turn I came up against resistance.
In the midst of my relatives, I found the absolute.
You told us to be like You, both out and inside holy,
In this world of many ways, You are the only truth.

At the end of the day, I wanted the soft option
To claim to be different ... and yet follow the crowd.
Instead of looking for an out, I should have asked You in,
And to Your timeless knowledge, let my pride be bowed.

Deborah A Davis

I AM

Touched by his love,
Healed by his hand,
Lead by his spirit,
Cradled by his arms,
Warmed by his voice,
Protected by his might,
Held in his palm,
Saved by his blood.

Sue Heyward

CRYING IN THE WILDERNESS

Listen! Anyone who does not know God.
Listen! Take away the tattered garment of an empty pride
From your heart.

Can man judge God,
Or criticise the will of his Creator?

Who are the Lord's people?
They are his jewels, his special possession,
His treasure.

In the day of his returning
They will be recognised before men.

Now, the world is upside down
With cumulated sin and great unrest,
But the Lord hears those who fear and talk of him,
Worshipping with reverential fear:
Of whom a book is kept
That is the Lord's, of every single one.

In that day, the Lord's name only will be exalted,
The Lord's name only will be exalted:
And the meek shall inherit the earth.

Ann Whitehouse

PRAYER FOR LOVED ONES

I thank you dear Lord
For your care this day,
Now that night has come
Hear me as I pray.

Hear my humble prayer
For those I love the Most,
Keep them in your care
Guarded by your heavenly host.

Give them your wondrous peace,
Show them that the heavenly way
To perfect joy and happiness
Is when they kneel and pray.

Show them how to love
And praise you every day,
That as a heavenly Father
You take all sin away.

When their eyes grow weary
And their earthly life is past,
Let them go with gladness
To your heavenly home at last.

J Brown

UNTITLED

A friend you are a friend you'll be,
but you do not belong to me.
There's someone else in your life.
I hope she'll never be your wife.
We go for drinks and meals too.
The time we spend together is short.
But who's to know where it will end,
or will you always be just my friend.

Jane Baxter

A FAMILY PRAYER

Our Father, God in heaven,
Bless us, the Dyer Family.
Lead us in the ways of goodness
and of righteousness.
So that we help and cherish one another in the joys of
family life.
We have been indifferent to You Lord.
We have not done Your will.
We have not done those things
Which we ought to have done.
Help us to be aware of our weaknesses, and erring
ways.
Make us strong and resolute in mind and spirit loving
You,
Who died for us, upon the cross.
We pray for our Dyer forefathers,
And for the Dyers not yet born.
Help us Lord Jesus to love You,
As You have loved us.

Frederick Dyer

IMAGINE

Imagine falling asleep with a beautiful dream
With visions of wonder like you've never seen,
And waking to find at last you are home
And through its pastures you freely roam.
Imagine a garden with the deepest green grass
With perfected peace that will never pass,
And beautiful colours so rich and so deep
And never wanting to awake from that sleep.
Imagine seeing a light shining bright
With perfect harmony always in sight.
And finding the loved ones waiting for you
And knowing what Jesus has done for you.
Imagine walking on the grounds of our Lord
With nothing to make that scene be ignored.
And knowing that you will never leave home
And knowing you'll never again feel alone.

Fiona Gilpin

AUTUMN MEMORIES

As autumn leaves fall on the ground,
All colours of greens, gold and brown,
Fires glowing in every room,
To take away the winter gloom,
I still remember
When we walked together,
That September day,
We were so happy, and in love,
We had so much to say.
That memory will stay with me
Until my dying day,
One thing they cannot take away,
Are memories that will always stay.

E J Green

31

HEART'S CRY

Last night, you took my husband to his rest
      and soothed away his pain,
Left me alone, my anguish on my face
      writ clear for all to see:
So Lord, stretch out Your hand and comfort me.

Last night, you took my husband in your arms
      gave him everlasting joy,
Left me alone, darkness enclosing me
      no path for me to see;
Oh Lord, stretch out Your hand and comfort me.

Tonight, I needs must start my life anew
      show me the way to go
As I'm alone, my Guide, my Mentor be
      my Light that I may see:
O Lord, be my friend and comfort me.

Peggy Netcott

THE ASS

Who is He I carry here?
With a kind voice
and lack of fear!
They travel far and near
to see his face,
we travel at a very slow pace.
I heard said, He makes
the blind to see and
the crippled walk,
Oh! Lucky me! to be in
such close proximity.

Kathy

UNTITLED

Our future King and Queen,
Are also human beings with feelings
of joy and pain - Anxieties and ills,
losses and gains.
In spite of the tie that binds
they are entitled to change their minds.

So many times love grows cold,
Despite duties one can't be bold,
To endure unhappiness or
live without a comforting caress
in the arms of our best friend,
why should they have to pretend.

The days are long gone by
when people live a lie and
then before too long of a broken
heart they die.
When love was strong and in bloom
They did become bride and
groom but when our lips grow
cold, the other should be told.
Life changes all the while
Let's face it with a smile
Take each day as it comes and ends
you will soon find another friend.

C E Leslie

GALLOWS HILL

They said: 'It's a place of suffering,
Of sorrow and sadness and sin,
Plague-dead were brought here for burial.'
'Yes! And a local man did himself in '
Archaeologists disputed the matter
Claimed the evidence didn't exist.
So I went to the hill late one evening
To consider the tales that I'd heard,
Curious, apprehensive and doubting,
Seeking proof that could be written in words.

I approached with a clamour of questions,
Unresponsive the hill remained mute.

Silent across the grass the evening shadows lay
Lengthening slowly with the slowly dying day.
Gentle the breeze and slight movement of leaves,
Infrequent call of small birds settling down to rest.
Then overall, the silence that falls at day's end,
When the sun goes to his quiet repose
Beyond the far hill.
And night comes and the moonlit sky,
And across the moon,
The veils of ghostly shadows fly.
I grew still in the silence and listened,
Felt in the motionless air,
An arrow-sharp moment of insight
Knew the pain and the suffering there.

Hilarie Perry

GOD'S CREATION

Who made you out of clay?
Moulding you each night and day,
It was our Father in every splendour
And give us all each night to remember,
Even the birds and bees of the air,
Know who their father is and cares
The trees that clap their hands so high
Bow down their heads because He's nigh,
they all know who their father is,
Because he greets each one to kiss
So lets remember all His creation
Of His wonders and salvation,
the animals that went two by two
On Noah's Ark was all so true,
The burning bush was all aflame
Has God shouted out His name.
And Joseph with his coat of many colours
Was so amazing to his brothers.
Let's not forget the might hand
that divided the sea for the Promised Land,
And when all this time went by,
The Father sent Jesus in the wing of an eye.
To Mary and Joseph came this child,
So precious and wonderful, meek and mild,
Then to a man that He did grow,
Walking the earth on which to sow
The work that through his Father came,
He did it all through flesh and name.
This name of Jesus means Emmanuel
For God is with us all is well...

Anita Heap

THE POPPIES

The poppies shone bright
      as the blood of man,
Who lies in a warrior's grave,
He died, he was only one of the many
That gave his life to save.

The poppies shone bright in
      Remembrance,
On that sad and awful day,
Of the soldier who gave his life
      for us,
That we on the earth might stay.
And though we are sad and sorry,
But yet our eyes shine bright,
Because of that man who gave his all
In that mightiest ever fight.

Edith Gash

LIGHT OF THE WORLD

Descending light upon the world,
Rays of blessed peace touch the earth.

Prayers that never go unheard
in this every changing universe.

Love and life
given to every living thing.

Heavenly choirs of angels sing
indeed these are the blessed things.

Christine Jackson

I LIE AWAKE

When in the night I lay awake
I think of God up in the heavens,
And ask and wonder why I should
Have suffered much and to what good.

My thoughts then go to 'Jesus Christ',
He suffered much and paid a price,
He did not sin like I have done,
But pain and agony he had to succumb.

He asked his 'Heavenly Father' for help,
His prayer was very earnest,
He knew it was the will of God
And so he bore the burden.

'Lord' help me to follow such a course,
And not ask why I should,
But know it is thy way, O Lord,
To lead me up above.

The 'Good Lord' spoke to me and said
I know your need my son,
One day you will understand it all
And never doubt My love for thee.

J H Bridgeman

THE GIFT OF POETRY

God speaks to those divinely spurr'd
To fashion images with words

*'However skilful your design
The gift of poetry is mine.'*

John Trevena

UNTITLED

I love you Lord Jesus
With every beat of my heart,
I loved you Lord Jesus right from the start,
When I was a child
As high as a chair,
I loved you Lord Jesus
And I knew you were there.
You led me and showed me
The rights and the wrongs,
Through life I tried to do what you taught me
But I strayed and I sinned
In growing up in life,
Until one day I became a wife
I had two children and a lot of strife,
But I always found you at times of stress,
You helped me and loved me and I found happiness,
And now I am old and content with my life,
For my true love has found you
And you are my life.
I love you Lord Jesus and always will,
You are beside me through thick and thin,
I love you Lord Jesus and I praise your name.

Amen.

G Carr

SHORT CUT TO FREEDOM

You would be wise
Not living on lies,
Whilst about you the world dost change.
A person not whole,
Without aim or goal,
Discovers that life's out of range.

Where a lunacy reigns
Are hidden deep pains
Madness but acts as a screen
Get out of the rut
Take freedom's short cut
Do something you really mean.

Chucunabhar

WHY IS MAN SO BLIND

God must be a wonderful man
To create all things
With the wave of his hand.

He gave beautiful colours
To the fish in the sea,
He created the sky
for the birds to be free.

He created all animals
In pairs to create,
And created man
With his woman as mate.

Somewhere along the way,
Something went wrong,
Because man fought wars
And invented the bomb.

It may be God's way
Of telling man,
Don't be like the ostrich
Take your head out the sand.

Bert Booley

I'M HOMELESS!

You can see me walking on the street,
you can't know how I feel,
walking, begging, praying too,
wondering where I'll get my next meal.
It's a frightening world
with new surprises
waiting for me,
when the sun rises.
Holes in my shoes,
corns on my feet,
never trusting the people
that I meet.
I pray for the next morning
I'll still be alive,
but I don't know how
much longer I can survive.
I've lost count of the beatings,
living on these streets,
I've lost count of the nights
I've cried myself to sleep.
Some people say 'Go home'
from them I run and hide,
I'm safer on the streets than there
and I've still got my pride.
Next time you walk down your street
and you hear my plea,
try to give, maybe sacrifice
to help someone like me.

Kelly Morris

WHAT IS A NATION?

Legends linger.
Floating about the mind
like half forgotten memories.
The past mingling with today.
Desperately trying to exist
on the crumbs of an old culture.
A banquet must be made of the new one.
Relishing its varieties, its textures and its flavours.
National regeneration cannot be founded on false mythology.
How do we distinguish
between mythology and truth?
The festering wounds of generations past.
Language and emotions trampled underfoot.
We are all His children -
Regardless of tongue or creed.

Iona James

THE GREAT CREATOR

God made the world so beautiful, adorning it with flowers
Which give the lives of you and me so many pleasant hours.
There are mountains, lakes, and pastures green,
And many a beauty spot to be seen;
With fields of corn that turn to gold
When kissed by the sun, a joy to behold.
The mighty sea gives up its fish
Which finish up as a tasty dish.
How can it be that some are blind
To God's creations for mankind?
It's a wonderful world in which we live,
So let all praise to our Maker give.

Sylvia Hills

REALITY

Dabble in scrabble, oh dear,
What a lot of dross I hear,
No matter the source through the medium,
TV, papers, people, tedium.

Sex, violence, drugs or booze,
God help the young not much to choose,
All so maudlin, near fatality,
No wonder I don't like reality,
Rise above it find vitality.

Stick to walks up paths through trees,
A little rain and a gentle breeze,
Enjoy the sunshine all natures treasures,
Simple things bring the greatest pleasure.

All life devours you, your brain and then your heart,
The miracle is to play your par,
Lift your eyes to the magnificent world,
Other cultures free in spirit
All God's gifts await therein it.

I lived a life of many guises
Lots of years to know the wisest,
At the end of the day it was still me,
Spiritual progress the way it has to be ...

Jean Tennent Mitchell

FALLING NATION

Once called the 'Great' British Empire,
    that was years ago;
A nation that burned with ambitious desire,
    now it's just a glow.
When will the Phoenix rise from the embers,
to fulfil the people's dreams?
To rebuild a nation as one remembers,
to quell political screams?
Governments rise, promises spoken,
their task, to rule the nation;
Governments fall, promises broken,
the people, left uncertain.
The nation once sparkled like a gemstone,
    like steel, now gathers rust.
We should have let God rule from his throne,
    at least in him we could trust.
At each other's throats, all seeking votes,
politicians, trying to get tough;
they bicker and stall, don't answer the call,
for the people, that isn't enough.
The poor are getting poorer, the weak are getting weaker,
even the sick, have no escape.
Some await the surgeons knife, to give them back a life,
but are denied, by mix-ups and red tape.
Crime is getting worse, underpaid doctor, nurse,
unemployment spreads like a disease;
the nation once stood tall, even I have seen it fall,
and sadly, brought down to its knees.

Firecloud

DEAD LETTERS

After the thunder and the shouts
Of the forgotten, stumbling out
Into a cavernous world,
Merging memory and dreams, hurled
To the ground like heavy loads
Cast from angry grey clouds ...

The stillness of silent doubts
In caves and rain-washed streets,
And the hours of fasting spent
On a Sabbath, worn-out by want
Of a creator, giving new breath
To the dead letters they loved with.

Then the opening of morning's
Sharp eye on the promised meanings
Found in the tomb's gaping black,
Like a puncture-hole in the wreck
Of a gaunt, stretched-out body ...

And day's beginning bathed in the bloody
Light of a wounded sun which rises
As a striding figure passes
From the sick clutches of the grave
Into the fierce arms of our lives.

Simon Stewart

TARRY FORTH COMPANION

Tarry forth companion, you will find truth one day,
Seek true friendship, work for your needs along the way,
Steer clear of idle souls and the traps of vanity and greed,
The spiritual road is straight, but of great need,
The burdens of life weigh heavy, they seek your special worth,
Precious gems, come from the pressures of the earth,
Actors learn their lines, before they play their part
A hand is holding yours, a test is on your heart.

T Allbright

GOD IS MY FRIEND

Often I wonder, what life is all about,
Sometimes I think I'm trapped and there's no way out.
Very often I feel lonely and long for a special friend,
One I can rely on, whose friendship will not end.
Many times in life, my heart has felt such pain,
I've cried so many many tears, that I felt I couldn't cry again.
But then the sadness never lasts that long, for my
heart fills with happiness, when I hear birds in full song.
How can I be trapped when I'm able to live free,
And see such beauty everywhere, such loveliness I see.
And how can I be lonely when I have God as my friend,
He listens to my troubles, on Him I can depend.
Tears I cry can be for happiness too, we have to
get on with life, we have God's work to do.
When I wake he's there alongside of me, when
I feel trapped he sets me free.
I want God as my lifelong companion, he
holds me in His warm embrace, for with
Him to hold and comfort me, the world's
a much friendlier place.

Melinda Evans

THOUGHTS ABOUT CHRISTMAS

Christmas used to be in December
With holly, cake and snow,
But now it comes in late summer
To help the stores' 'cash flow'.
As a child I liked the fun
Of opening all my presents,
Eating turkey, stuffing and black bun
Guessing then what I might get
Not sleeping on Xmas Eve.
One year I asked for a pet
How Santa did deceive!
Now it's just a nightmare
As I start to save my pennies,
The kids want computer ware,
Debts become a menace,
So, dear Jesus, up above
Could you come down soon,
And show again, it's a time for love
And not asking for the moon!
And so I've decided in September
To revive your message of love,
I'll forget the shops and just remember
Why you came down from above.

Moira Michie

CHRISTMAS BABY

A great celebration,
So long as we remember to put Christ first.
It is easy to be so busy,
That we forget the baby, born
In a stable,
The Son of God.

Jennifer Adams

GOING RUSTY

I have now reached the age of creak and groan
and all I seem to do is moan,
it's all to do with getting old
my poor old bones are always cold.

Fruit is tastier when it's ripe, 'tis said,
I feel over ripe as I trundle to bed.
But tomorrow is another day.
I must awake, please God I pray.

Maturing years should be trouble free
But no feel good factor I can see.
I wish I could be born again
And set me free from all this pain.

But some are good things now I'm old
As long as I do as I'm told,
Don't call the doctor out at night,
But go to him if walk I might.

We ride on buses with fare paid.
Front seats especially for concessions made,
Theatre's too are cheaper with a Pension Book
and you don't mind matinees, it's worth a look.

But life is sweet if our health is good
and before we end in our coat of wood,
let's thank God that we've lived so long,
we'll sing out loud 'till our final song.

I wouldn't really change a thing,
I'll wear life now like, my old wedding ring,
I can't believe my hair's now white,
I'm as old as I feel, so I'll wish you goodnight!

G Edwards

DO YOU BELIEVE

Do you believe there's a destiny for all,
Our fate in God's hands until he does call,
We're here for a reason some would say,
Believe in God he will show you the way.

Do you believe in Adam and Eve,
Some people find them hard to perceive,
They never existed some would say,
But people get scared keep the unknown at bay.

Do you believe in Jesus Christ,
A man of such purity, a man without vice,
He's the son of the Lord some would say
Spreading the word of God, bringing a brighter day.

And what of God himself I ask,
Does he really set us all a task,
If things go wrong it's 'God's will' they would say,
And if there is evil, he'll make you pay.

What do I believe you ask,
I believe my destiny is vast,
I really don't care what they would say,
For if God put me here it's to do it my way!

Jacqueline Griffiths

CHRISTMAS

Christmas time is the time for me
The fairy lights upon the tree,
Glittering stars in children's eyes
As they unwrap another surprise,

All relaxed having a drink
Pots piled high in the sink
Enjoying games, we all can play
How I love Christmas Day,

My door is open, friends come in,
Happiness is all you need to bring
Christmas songs we all enjoy,
Remembering the birth of that little boy,

And when everyone has gone home
Memories I have, I'm never alone,
Sleep tonight with peace of mind,
Were you good, were you kind?
Goodnight, God bless, sleep tight,
Dream of Santa, he came last night.

J Taylor

LORD - YOU KNOW BEST

When all of life's problems seem too heavy to handle,
Or all of life's joys seem to be passing me by,
I sit down and wonder, 'Lord, what's going on?'
But He bids me, 'Come . . . and don't question, *why?*
I'll show you some splendours I have in My word -
Come! Listen to Me, there's lots to be heard.'
And so I say, 'Yes, I'll spend time with You.'
Then, earth's treasures vanish for heaven's in view.
'Take your eyes off your problems, place your focus on Me.
Hand over your worries and I'll set you free.
For you know this, my child - life's not full of fun
But with Me by your side, the battles'll be won!
For I paid the price to set your soul free.
Don't rely on yourself - trust only in Me.'

Glory to Jesus
Lift high His name
Praise Him forever
He's always the same!

Elizabeth Hillan

SIGNS OF SPRING

The grey clouds stand still
in the overcast sky.
The stark hedgerows wait, for the
first showing of their new mantle.

On the still air a blackbird
heralds the coming of the
long awaited spring.
The banks in the sunken lane,
are springing to life.
Sheltered from the raw winds,
that blow across the fields.

The browned grass offers little feed
to the small lambs gambolling round.
Awaiting the plaintiff cry
of mother searching them.
High above carrion crows circle
looking for titbits left at lambing time.

Sheltered on the banks,
celandines are growing in profusion.
Giving a promise of better things
to come, as spring takes hold.
As it surely will.

Peter Isles Orr

TREASURES OF THE MIND

Treasure daybreak when you open your eyes,
the heaven above beauty of the skies.
Starting the day to riches galore,
Recording each moment, the mind to store.

Treasure the laughs, friends meeting together,
A memory or two recalled in measure.
Quietly sitting remembering a smile,
That brightened the day for awhile.
Cherish with care thoughts in the mind,
Kindness and love, with support combined.

Treasure the faces, in frames, forever,
The happy times shared together.
Wishing to see with all our worth,
Loved and revered while here on earth.
Thinking with such intensity,
Never forgetting till eternity.

Treasure the smile of your child abounding.
A gift given with love astounding.
Appreciate all things as we pass by
The world revolves and days will fly.
God's earth is such a wonderful place,
Treasures given to all in His good grace.

Ivy E Baker

ODE TO A BROTHER

'Don't forget to remember me'
Are some words from a song
But while your memory is so vivid
You'd not stray from my mind for long.

We had no warning you were going away,
To be seated at God's right side,
At the age of 17½, we thought you would live
For ever and a day.

We had our scraps, as siblings do
And probably drove mam mad,
But you had such a gentle nature too,
I was so glad of the years we had.

Intelligent, witty, articulate too,
Are some of the words to describe you,
You played the guitar so well, I thought,
I was listening to one of the records you bought.

On December 7th at about 8.30,
You left all hale and hearty,
To go to London and buy some clothes
For a 21st birthday party.

The day you died, the tears they flowed,
The neighbourhood were so very kind,
They held a collection down the road,
You were etched on everyone's mind.

I wish I could stand on the moon,
And reach up to heaven above,
To let you know we'll be together, however soon,
All I can do until then, is pledge my undying love.

God Bless and keep you safe.

Elaine Carver

THE GLASTONBURY THORN

Once, when ships could sail into Glastonbury,
In old rough rural and crude cruel days,
Witches and Wizards with fireworks and fury,
Devilish dances and weird wanton ways
Used such farce to enforce their power
And made poor superstitious souls cower.

Trade brought Joseph of Arimathaea,
Accompanied, legend says, by Our Lord,
And his planted staff made your blooms appear
From Jerusalem thorn on some steep sward;
An action that God might have planned
To make England more like The Holy Land.

Near Arthur's stronghold Isle of Avalon,
Your hill became God's Abbey Church terrain;
There your white wreaths each Christmas dawn
Reminded all of Christ's earthly reign,
Good life, true teachings, crucifixion pain,
Ascension, Grace and Coming Again.

Was it Church or State that burned your boughs?
Did King Hal's resolve to wed in a hurry
Decree your death and dissolve God's house
That in haste he might divorce and remarry?
Did Cromwell's Cavaliers your life's sap stay,
Believing their actions were heaven's way?

But sions saved by gardener's arts,
And set by 'Grail' seekers with gentle hearts,
Grew your Gospel message in secret parts,
Defeating the wills of those bold upstarts.
This poet, finding one of these places,
Near Saint John's Church, now writes your praises.

Ends.

Ronald Rodger Caseby

HOLY WAR - HOLY SMOKE SCREEN

Throughout the world religions are rife,
There are dozens of tenets to guide one's life,
Each of them teaches to love and to give,
Thou shalt not kill - help people to live.
It's noble to be poor and blessed to be meek,
Righteousness and purity is what we should seek.

Each of these sects has a figure to lead,
Only his teachings are what one should heed,
Live as he tells us - not as he does,
Believe in God's mercy yet fear punishment from above,
Be tolerant to all men and help those in need,
But brook no argument if they question your creed.

A Catholic loves his neighbour, does he not,
As long as he is not one of that Protestant lot.
Muslims love one another and me and you,
Providing of course we are none of us a Jew,
Hindus are gentle and love all mankind
Except for a Sikh for he's a different kind.

It seems not to matter what denomination,
Each is determined to achieve domination,
These leaders of men are so held in awe,
That their followers rally when they cry 'Holy War',
But on analysis it can be clearly seen,
Their implorings are more of a 'Holy Smoke Screen'.

Alan Nicholls

ST MARY'S CHURCH, HARBY

It is a delight to visit St Mary's Church,
where the door is open every day,
one can meditate and pray.

There to welcome you,
as you open the door, is
a pedestal of beautiful flowers
beckoning you, to come inside,
for you will find
tranquillity and peace
silence! One with God.
A haven, from the busy world.

A bible is open in the children's corner
pictures drawn with eager hands
by children, longing
to hear the stories of Jesus and
sing praises to our Lord.

So well kept the twinkling brass
the altar cloths white as snow.
Kneeling hassocks deftly sewn
by loving hands.
For this is 'God's' home.
So pleasant are the parishioners
greeting you with a smile
as the church bells ring
all unite and sing the rector
praying for peace and thanking
God for everything.

Gladys Davenport

DON'T LOOK - LISTEN

It's me in here I want to shout
At people who poke fun
Look at her how does she cope
She must weigh half a ton
If I could be just half my size
They wouldn't even look
Or make those cruel and nasty jokes
And treat me like a crook.

Think thin they try to tell me
And you will loose that weight
Exercise and go for walks
Keep busy ... You won't eat
I've tried all this to no avail
And when I stop to think
It doesn't matter anyway.

My family don't give a damn
My friends think I'm O.K.
I will not let it worry me
It will not make me ill
So mind your business, keep out your nose,
You are not welcome here.

Sue Flower

COME, HOLY SPIRIT

Spirit of God, descend
       And dwell within my heart.
My selfish longings end
       And purify each part.

Spirit of Christ, arrive
       And live within my soul.
Make my spirit come alive
       And take complete control.

Spirit of Holiness, come
 And take up Your abode.
Make myself Your home
 And remove the awful load.

Spirit of peace, reside
 Within my troubled breast.
With You I would abide
 And in You find my rest.

R A Davis

SOON

Soon this toilsome life I'll finish,
soon a better land I'll know,
soon I'll cease this daily labour,
say farewell to all below.

When my name the Master whispers,
saying, 'Come home, David, son,
your first term of life has ended
and your work on earth is done.'

Day by day my Saviour guides me,
helping me, my load to bear,
and I long to sing His praises
in that land beyond compare.

But, my friend, would you be ready
if you heard the trumpet blow?
Telling all that He's returning
as He promised long ago.

If not, why won't you try Jesus?
He will take you by the hand,
lead you through these troubled waters
to that glorious heavenly land.

McCullough Templepatrick

EAGLES

To soar upon the wing where eagles glide,
My heart to rejoice,
To fly over mountains that were deep inside.

To be free and touch the sun,
Flying through clouds of purest white,
Oh my Lord my life begun.

To be master of the winds,
To fly through valleys of emerald green,
Such beauty my Lord, to my eyes you bring.

Soaring over cascading waterfalls,
The colours of the rainbow, as waters melt to mighty river,
For now the beckoning of horizons calls.

To be free from all of man's pains,
And sorrowful captivities,
The joys of soaring freedom remains.

Oh to glide upon the wing,
To be with Jesus, to be a king,
My longing to be an eagle,
Forever deep within,

                      Amen

Derek Thompson

LOVE

'Twas when I was feeling very low the
     children flown the nest
that I longed for a companion this
     idea was my best
I searched through all the adverts
     within my local mail
when my eyes were drawn to one
     which certainly I would nail.
Keen for a first meeting it proved
     love at first sight
a strong good-looking companion
     for me was just right.
To put up with my singing a' soon
     as doors close
My voice often echoes around
     English roads.
We share control of most things
     though mine is the 'upper hand'
I love to have surprises so our
     life is never planned
This friend holds all my heart strings
     and is never very far,
a companion true and constant
     You've guessed, it is
     My car!

Olive Bedford

59

A DAY AT A TIME

Treat each day as a separate unit,
This is difficult to do.
Never let tomorrow's problems
Into this day with you.
The scriptures say (in effect!)
'Live one day at a time'
This way you will find
Peace of mind -
So - seek His way at the
Start of each day;
Make Him your Friend
Now - and to the end!

Patricia Lawrence

HE IS ALWAYS THERE

When you have wandered away from the fold
And the things of the world weigh you down.
Your life seems in pieces, your heart feels so cold,
There is darkness and gloom all around
Look up to the heavens and call on the Lord
For strength to carry you through.
His love will enfold you and protect you from harm,
He will help you weather the storm.
Remember, His love is unfailing and true,
There is no-one more special than you.
He knows all your worries, your cares and your
woes,
Your burdens He gladly will bear.
Just lift up your eyes, your heart and your voice
And call on the Lord. He'll be there.

Jan Hellberg

COMPASSION OF THE LORD

The Lord said love one another.
Love is the thing that should help all Christian
People to support each other so that we can
Stand firmly together in the service of Jesus.

You will find the most important lesson about
Prayer is not just asking for what you want!
It's also a time for thanking God,
And for feeling compassion when you see
Others in trouble.

The story of Jesus, and the way He dealt with
A deaf man who cam seeking a cure for
His deafness. Jesus took him to one side
Away from the crowd to spare him embarrassment.
For He chose to heal him in private.
You see people mattered to Jesus, even the
Humblest of men, they still do!

Ken Pendlebury

A JOURNEY HOME

When day is done and we say goodbye,
We can never understand why,
As we leave loved ones in tears behind,
We move along seeking peace every soul must find,
Now we sail a ship on another sea,
A voyage filled with hope for new discovery,
So when our journey ends at that lighted shore,
We are welcomed by all who have gone on before,
Those people we loved and voices from the past,
Sing joyful songs we are home at last.

Joan Willson

YOU ARE NEVER ALONE

You may not feel God's presence
as you flounder on your way,
Bent low with tiresome trials,
Struggling another step to take;
But God is *always* with you,
In joy as well as pain,
His shoulders ever ready
to support you through the strain.
He sees each tear that trickles,
He hears the plaintive sigh;
He is watching o'er you *always*
and will *never* overload.

To Him you are most special
and He is working to enhance
the life that He has given:
You can trust the Creator's hand.
If you listen for His voice,
You will hear Him softly say -
'My child, I love and prize you,
I have made and I will bear.
I am with you *always,*
I will *never* you forsake.
My peace I give unto you
I plan good for you, not evil.'

Shirley Hay

HE KNOWS BEST

We sometimes scorn life's station
That God has placed us in.
We long to do some wondrous work
To please and honour Him;
Yet He it is who chose the place
And set our hands to plough
The furrows of the untouched earth
Of hearts that need Him, now!
Perhaps without our caring prayers
For those within our sphere
They would never come to know
His love, and feel Him near.
So tend with care His chosen plot,
He'll guide and show the way,
Amazingly, through Spirit's power
Comes victory as we pray.
And tho' our work be commonplace
Perhaps unseen by man,
The God of grace who placed us there
Knows His mighty plan.
This should be enough to know
That someone has to do
The everyday, unnoticed work
To bring His glory through.
So in the unseen realms of life
Take courage in the task,
Remembering Him who chose us
To be faithful to the last.

Elizabeth Bruce

UNTITLED

In this world of confusion,
I turn my heart to Thee.
For Thou art the shadow of my soul.
I have lit the candle to my inner self
and my world unfolds.
In my heart peace and contentment rushes,
to the forefront, bringing tears to my eyes.
Now is the time to live in my new world
and not behind my discontentment of lies.
You are in my every breath,
Each step I take, I only wish to please Thee.
Your light shineth down upon me to lighten
my darkness, all my fears cease,
O faithful loving God, I am peace,
                              I am peace.

P S Hunt

BY OUR FAITH

They do not see, nor yet perceive.
They do not hear, nor understand.
But by our faith do we believe
And speak Your truths throughout the land.

Their eyes are closed and will not see.
To deafened ears Your word imparts.
But we receive Him joyfully
With understanding in our hearts.

Lord, let us bring sight to their eyes
And let them hear what we have heard.
For every soul should realise
The power in the Saviour's word.

Andrew Jones

GOD

You speak to me of God, you ask where He is?
I answer He is everywhere,
but you don't understand.
So I tell you, He is all around you in everything you see,
and even in those things you do not see
You then ask me why has He turned away from me?
I answer, it was you who turned away from God.
You ask will God help me?
I say yes, if you ask unselfishly.
But remember, God helps those who help themselves,
and in order to help yourself,
you must put others before yourself,
then you will see God's Kingdom!

Remember God's wisdom is love!

R T Clark

FOREVER THERE

You must prepare yourself for your new life
with righteous deeds right now.
Begin to see the continuation of all things
that should be,
forever here, forever there.
Always there, always here.
Entwined together in a twisted dilemma
of movement in action;
of thoughtful creation,
that eventually through stillness
opens our eyes
to the answer that is forever there.

G C Heath

THE SEASONS

In spring our hearts are lightened
By tho myotorioo of oarth.
Sweet flowers the world has brightened
The air is full of mirth.

The daffodils are golden
Bringing joy for all to share.
The vivid scarlet tulips
And lilac sweet and fair.

Summer days pass quickly by
Flowers bloom in gardens fair.
Roses, lilies, columbine
Shedding fragrance everywhere.

Autumn with its colours bold
Makes a change on every hand.
Reds and browns and greens and gold
Picturesque, a wonderland.

Then, alas, on wintry days
Snug beside the fireside glow.
Threatening clouds, and boisterous winds
Hail and frost and pure white snow.

At the closing of the year
Birds have gone and trees are bare
Christmas comes with all its cheer
Goodwill and joy is everywhere.

Freda M Walker

PRAYER

Trembling hands clasped for prayer
Ready to take comfort from
All that I fear.

For my Lord will listen
And show me the way.
For His love is eternal
And shines brighter
Each day.

Strength gained from prayer
Displays faith in my eyes.
No need for deception
No need for lies.
Each time I kneel
Fanfares fill the skies.
For those who feel
Something is missing
There is no need to
Scream and shout.
For the power of prayer is
Unequalled of which I
Have no doubt.

R Clarke

HAVE FAITH

When you are feeling bad and the skies are grey
Lift up your eyes at the end of the day
There is help to cope waiting there
Trust in Him who is full of care
He will uplift your heart with comfort and love
The One who cares most
Your Father above.

Evelyn A Evans

HAVE YOU? HAVE I? HAVE WE?

Have you been under stresses and strains - felt restless, tired and drained?
Have you been under some of life's heavy burdens   with bridges to cross
over again?
Have you to cope with family problems - with that responsible job -
with responsibility to you?
Have you experienced personal grief, and the sorrow that follows you
through?
Have you forgiven yourself and others - for times when we knew not what
we do?
Have you taken the blame for something done, because of another person's
self-pride being strong?
Have we to take up courage - not be afraid - to clear our personal name
from wrong?
Have we really need to create, the many afflictions on one another, in our
lives and living?
Have you felt the loving spirit of Christmas peace - which should be all
year round, in its giving?
Have you felt upset over problems human beings make - past and present -
over our different shades of skin?
Have you thought why God did this - when knowing human nature ways
and sins?
Have we got to learn with understanding - how very different we have been
born in many ways?
Have we only to receive God's holy spiritual love - use it personally
throughout our living days?
Have we to organise time for ourselves - a few minutes' silence - ways to
recharge our cells?
Have we to take a rest from our labours - and our neighbours - find time
for ourselves to unwind?
Have we to use meekness, mercy and kindness in our service for God
and mankind?

Daphne May Cutler-Allum

SEARCH AND FIND

All those years that I was blind
I searched and searched but could not find,
A lasting joy, a peace that would stay
For more than a week, a month, or a day
I thought the world could give me it all
But then one day I heard the Lord call
Repent and I'll cleanse you and free you from sin
I stand here and knock please let me come in
Give me your heart come follow me
I'll give you a peace and a joy you'll see
Troubles and problems may still appear
But I'll be there with you never fear
God is all powerful He is everywhere
He loves us so much He really does care
Share the gospel salvation is free
It's true Jesus died for you and for me
Life is unpredictable please don't wait
Accept God's gift now before it's too late.

W Barrett

BEST FOOT FIRST

Reaching out, into space,
I put forward my case!
Are we facing in, or are we facing out?
Where should I begin?
Doesn't anyone know,
Can't anyone show me the way to go?
So on stellar winds I could flow,
Out into space
And look the Almighty in the face . . .
To put forward my case!

John Downing

THE ANGELS SING HOLY HOLY!

Lord, I love the silence, the silence that You bring.
The waves of peace that come, awesome stillness, deep within.
Love, so unconditional, one weeps with tears of joy!
Oh, the wonder of Your faithfulness, in the face of sin.
Astonishment at such a love, a holy God suspended on a cross.
A mind that planned a life given freely, all for us.
Life-giving words 'Yes, I will, be thou healed!'
Truth and grace and mercy so lovingly revealed.
He has shewn the path, His hand beckons 'Come walk with Me!'
There is a path of beauty where restoration flows for you - just see!
But child, can you die to all you want to be?
The meekest in all the earth - our God, walked this path, great glory, great
power,
in sacrificial love.
To shine, thro' any darkness, to overcome the worst Satan can bring.
Is this not a calling to make the angels sing!

Mary Comley

TASTE OF PARADISE

To touch the intangible
Speak the ineffable
See the invisible
Hear the inaudible
Smell the imperceptible
Is to draw near to
My God in paradise,
Even in Calcutta's gutters,
Come, taste the tree of life.

Len Fishenden

70

NO MAN IS AN ISLAND

No man is an island
No man stands alone
There is always someone
Near to you, to help you when you're down.

Someone who will give a smile
Or a cheering word
Someone who will listen
And not pass on what they've heard.

It may be a loved one
Or a stranger in the street
Just someone who is there
Who that day you chance to meet.

Or it may be the spirit
Of someone who's gone before
Who has come back to help you
Through heaven's golden door.

It doesn't really matter
Who your helper may be
For when they've passed by
You'll realise, life's not as black as it seemed to be.

So greet each stranger with a smile
For you may ease his burden.
And you will feel better for that
Of that you can be certain.

Valerie Lloyd

PRAYER FOR TODAY

Lord another day has dawned
draw near as I kneel to pray
touch me with Thy healing hand
and give me strength for this new day

guard me with Thy presence Lord
so I can stand the strain
against the trials and the strife
against the thought of worldly gain

let not my heart be hardened Lord
or my eyes be blind that I cannot see
and help me take the stress of life
with a new strength only found in Thee

with your love to guide me
I can face the day
be Thou my guard and shield
when trouble comes my way

when the battle rages
let my faith in You be strong
till the battle's over
and another victory won

Frank Scott

XMAS DAY

A Baby born on Xmas Day
A Baby in a stable lay
Sent by the Lord of Hosts above
To bring His people home with love

Love enfolds this Xmas Day
The Babe our hope to show the way
Shepherds watching flocks at night
Up in the sky a star so bright

72

A message sent by God in Heaven
This Xmas Day new hope is given
A world in peace we hopeful pray
A Babe is born this Xmas Day

So joyous sing and all unite
In peace and love this Xmas night
Watched over by the Lord above
Who sent his Son with hope and love

Mary Hudson

A CHILD'S FIRST SIGHT OF THE SEA

These barren sands,
windswept morose and wide,
Covered low this stormy autumn day,
Meandering through rock and spray and tide,
Choosing shells and pebbles on the way.

A child of two,
wellies, hood and eyes,
In daddy's arms looks out across the brine,
An infant's grasp that helps him realise,
The qualities and richness of this time.

Can joy so deep,
Be nothing more than chance,
Mere union of cells and DNA,
Or is it more than fanciful romance,
To feel the work of grace in us this day.

If God there be,
In sea and rain and cloud,
I sense him here entrusted in my arms,
His presence makes me want to shout aloud,
As baby stares towards the distant Farnes.

Ian Petrie

CONFESSION

How hard to surrender, when once you've backslid,
How hard to admit that you've failed.
Once I came to the Lord, from my burden was rid,
Knew for certain His truth had prevailed.

How hard to return from the dark paths of sin -
How hard to admit that I'd failed;
His Spirit was yearning once more to come in
And proclaim that His truth had prevailed.

How hard was committing my life once again;
How hard to admit I had failed.
The Saviour was seeking my life to reclaim
And to find that His truth had prevailed.

But His yoke is easy, His burden is light
To those who admit they have failed;
Again I've returned from sin's terrible night
And believe that His truth has prevailed.

Dear Saviour, I came and knelt down at Your feet
As I freely admitted I'd failed;
For with penitent heart, there at Your mercy seat
I confessed that Your truth had prevailed.

Once more I've committed my life unto Thee
But this time I know I won't fail;
Your cross is before me, Your presence goes with me,
In the future, Your truth *will* prevail!

Gail Shepherd

THINK FOR A BIT!

Think about Christmas this Christmas
Think about what it's all for
Repeats on the telly
An overstuffed belly
Too drunk to get up from the floor.
Mr Barnet, my neighbour's still lonely
His son never bothers to write
They say it's a time for goodwill to all men
But I'll still hear him crying tonight.

Think about Jesus this Christmas
Think about His humble birth
Prince of Peace, the Messiah,
Not a cheat, thief or liar,
He came down to bring peace on earth.
But brother still wants to kill brother
The answer they think, is to fight
'Do unto others - before they do you'
And you'll still see them dying tonight

Think about *Easter* this Christmas
Think about Christ on the tree
The love that He offers
to cynics and scoffers
And unworthy sinners like me.
The tree that He hung from was different
No tinsel, no baubles, no light
If you ask Him right now to come into your life
They'll be singing in Heaven tonight!

Val Bull

THOUGHTS IN ST MARGARET'S

(Thy hands have made me and fashioned me . . . Psalm 1119)

On entering St Margaret's church absorbed by atmosphere;
My mind regressed and thoughtful mused what workmanship is here.
Glancing; in a twinkling one sees richness in work untold,
And if this lovely church could speak what secrets she would unfold . . .
She would tell of sculptors' and stonemasons' skills
As around sandstone pillars one sees
From the ivy and oak to a fine sycamore, six delicate garlands of leaves.
Then we would hear of the pulpit, styled on the Gothic line,
Deep-cutting with intricate patterns; what beauty from sulphate of lime!
Would she then speak of the carpenters, who carved so exquisitely,
Angels and lions in fine choir stalls shielded by trellis worked painstakingly?
Should we hear next of the roof filled with oak, planed and chiselled with
care;
Cut, marked and measured with dextrous art? Surely God's presence
was there!
The rood screen too she would speak of, hammered fine, protective and tall;
Centred high crucifix of one who forgave; a poignant reminder for all!
The east window she would certainly mention with sun 'tis transformed to
a cloth,
And gives this scene three dimension; all to the glory of God!
Of other stained windows I feel she would tell depicting scenes Holy and
good
And the artists who gave of a lifetime to have toiled with what they
understood.
Then she would mention the paintings;
Revealing expressive and sensitive tones, unsurpassed beauty captured
As brightness from windows is thrown.
Last we would hear of makings in brass, from which processional and
altar cross grew,
Significant lectern and offertory plate, superb walled engravings etched too.
With thoughts still deep I turned to leave and knew God's hand was there;
What a legacy those craftsmen left by their labour, skill and care!

Brenda Davies

GOOD FRIDAY

Tomorrow is Good Friday
the stained day of the year
the day crucified,
Host shrouded, He died.
Temple doors wrenched
torn off their hinges
by a gale of anger.

Where are the marks
of this spring death?
Scourged, mocked and nailed,
only up that slope
Veronica's cool hands comforted,
and before Mary Magdalene.
Vinegar on a sponged stick,
a mouth that is too dry
for words except to gasp
let it pass.

The thief un-nailed on his cross
understood and knew
how great Your sacrifice,
that kiss of betrayal
the flash of Peter's sword
we never saw but are told.
We shroud ourselves
and only after Easter
take out the bent headed
daffodils from cherished vases
and then remember
Christ died.

Alan P Graham

PENTECOST

'Come Holy Spirit and baptise
As you did at Pentecost,
For people are gathered and waiting
As they did in days of old.
Some are uncertain and timid
And some are full of fear,
Some keep trying and failing
To walk in God's Holy ways,
And some are sick and weary
And struggle every day.

All of us need to be filled
With your power and sustaining might,
To be baptised with love
And put uncertainty to flight.

So come Holy Spirit come,
Fill each of us anew,
That in Your strength
We may go out
To share God's love
With people far and near.'

Pauline Holmes

THE HOPE AND ANCHOR

It didn't have a dartboard
It didn't serve a brunch,
It didn't have a weekly quiz,
Or sell a ploughman's lunch.

It didn't have a disco,
Its walls were dark and smoky,
It didn't have a kid's room
Or even karaoke

It didn't have a stripper,
I couldn't understand it,
It didn't have real beer
Or a shiny one-armed bandit

But as I left that evening
A star lit up the sky
And I saw it had a stable,
And I heard a baby cry!

Peter Davies

A HAPPY NEW YEAR

'A Happy New Year,' I said to myself as I waited for it to begin
Another new year, I thought, and I wondered what
this coming year would bring.
I watched the TV, heard Big Ben chime, and I thought of the year now past,
'A Happy New Year,' someone called, and I thought
'Well it can't be much worse than the last.'

I recalled New Year's Eve when I was a girl
standing at our open front door,
Up on the hilltop the church bells would chime
Answered down in the valley below by factory hooters,
and ships on the Tyne
Such a wonderful, welcoming din;
With our 'first foot' we'd join hands and sing 'Auld Lang Syne'
That's the way a New Year should begin.

But I looked to the future, not just to the past
there must be a better tomorrow
For men of good will have realised at last
We can't live on hatred and sorrow.
So let us all hope for a Happy New Year
and pray that all killing will cease.
Wouldn't it be wonderful to wake up and find
That our lovely old world was at peace.

Hannah M French

THOUGHTS ON GOOD FRIDAY

See the new lambs play
Admire the sunny day
Holidays have come
With few thoughts for *that one*
Who caused this day to be
A rest for you and me

Chocolate eggs and yellow chicks
The connection rarely clicks
Play some sport or watch the same
Never thinking of *that name*

Spring and Easter mean life's new
A special life was given for you
Pause just once and think today
Jesus died on Good Friday

Jeannette Facchini

CHRISTMAS TIME

C hildren performing the nativity
H oping mums and dads will see!
R eceiving Christmas cards from old chums
I t's great fun to remember everyone
S inging carols from door to door
T aking time to think who they are for
M ince pies and a glass of sherry
A ll help make us merry!
S tars shining brightly in the sky above
T hey remind me of Jesus' love
I open my eyes on Christmas Day
M ake my way to church to pray - that's
E xactly what Christmas time means to me!

Elaine Duggan

NEW YEAR'S EVE

So many memories at the closing of the year,
Time for reflection whilst in nostalgic mood,
Heartbeats quicken at mind's reminiscences,
Trembling I remembered the flowering of love.

As your eyes met mine, a strange sensation
Flooded my whole being, a wave of emotion
Swept over me, and though but an instant
Your gaze held mine, it seemed an eternity.

Then the moment of wonder at love's dawning,
Conceived anew as though for the first time,
The poignant memory I shall vividly remember,
As with clarity scenes of childhood endure.

At last the dream became for me the reality,
Long after recognition of my love for you,
Our first long-awaited conversation arose,
Eyes had expressed what our lips now sought.

With what candour we confided in one another,
Our sympathies being very closely in tune,
From that moment on images haunted my mind,
Deeply aware of all the words we had spoken.

Then love came in all its strength and force,
To gaze and confide were not nearly enough,
Nature not content until all passion spent,
Inexorably we drew towards the final ecstasy.

As this significant year draws to its close,
Now that we know all there is to be known,
Love's mysteries that were so fully revealed,
What was, remains, what lies ahead, unknown.

Betty Mealand

THE CHRISTMAS STORY

Long long ago a baby was born
We celebrate His coming on Christmas morn
In Bethlehem, the miracle of God's only Son's birth
Sent from Heaven to be Lord and Saviour on earth
We remember Mary and Joseph, a manger and oxen stall
The shepherds and wise men, we remember it all
We remember too, this very special Babe
Is the greatest gift to man, God has made
For 2000 years the wondrous story has been told
Rejoice that still today God's promises hold.

Audrey Myers

EASTER DAY

Easter morn dawned fine and bright
Some rain had fallen during the night.
Daffodils in their golden glory
Seemed to proclaim the Easter story.
I went to church at the usual time,
Just a few minutes after nine,
And what a delight it was to see
So many people in church with me.
All were there with just one thought,
To worship God, they way they ought
And rejoice at the rising of our Lord
Our voices raised with one accord.
Then the vicar speaking so sincerely
Helping us to see our Lord more clearly.
The organist playing as one inspired
The choir responding as required.
I shall not forget this Easter Day
As faithfully I wend my way.

Lilian Naisbitt

ADVENT

When Advent comes, we like to shop.
    We buy all sorts of things.
We need good presents, food and pop,
    Enough for rogues and kings.

But best of all, the cards we see
    And choose, as we prepare
To praise our Lord's nativity,
    Show others that we care.

A big card for posh aunty Molly.
    Small cards for those whom we meet.
The kids get snowmen and holly.
    The verses are thoughtful and neat.

Address and stamp them. Seal them up,
    And get them to the post.
With joy we'll walk - we'll take the pup.
    Then home for tea and toast.

The days are so short and so dark.
    The fairy lights are lit.
And early morning dogs, all bark
    As cards land on the mat.

Rush to open them with joy.
    The bright and cheerful glow
Of cards from granddad, Jill and Roy,
    And friends from years ago.

We hang them safely on the wall.
    It gives us such a thrill,
To put up cards from all
    Whom we know love us still.

Marj Norton

EASTER MORNING

Before dawn's light across the garden spread
Mary arose and made her way towards the tomb.
The mist of early morning lay across her path
No ray of hope and joy could shine through all her gloom.

But as she nearer came to the appointed place
Where Jesus' body had been laid to rest,
It seemed the massive stone had rolled away
Her heartbeat quickened and fear filled her breast.

Hurrying away, to Peter and to John she came
Shaking with grief and fear, she told what she had seen,
The tomb was open, Jesus' body gone;
She scarce could fathom in her mind what this might mean.

There were the cloths in which Jesus had lain.
Peter and John went in, and saw them lying there,
Believing, they returned to their own home
Only the weeping Mary stayed, in sad despair.

But as she weeping stood, with grief and woe cast down
She saw two shining angels, deep within the tomb,
They turned to tell her that her Lord was risen,
That resurrection joy had now dispelled the gloom.

And then she heard a voice, calling to soothe her fears.
She did not recognise the well-loved, the familiar voice,
But then when he had called her name, 'Mary!'
'Master' she answered. In glad joy her heart rejoiced.

Mary Johnson-Riley

NEW DAWN

I was full of despair this morning,
When the world was cold and grey,
My heart was sad and lonely,
And my feet were feet of clay;
Life had lost its purpose,
Too many things had gone wrong,
Tired of chasing rainbows,
Clinging to hopes that had gone;
I was full of despair this morning,
But I found as the time went by,
That the tick of the clock, so constant,
Was comforting to my mind;
Then the light crept in at the window,
The birds were beginning to sing,
And the sounds of the new day starting,
Seemed to give me more courage within;
Life renewed its challenge,
With so many things yet to do,
And I thought of the age-old motto,
'Unto thine own self be true'
So I stood and looked through the window,
At the early morning sky,
And I saw the trees, and the garden,
And I no longer wanted to cry;
My heart was filled with hope anew,
For life hadn't really begun,
And my spirits lifted and soared in me,
With the rise of the morning sun.

Dorothy Neil

HARVEST'S MESSAGE

In Tavistock I went along
On Harvest Thanksgiving day
To church, and heard an old man
Preach a message for today.

He asked us all to hear the Word
From God, who gives us all,
And then to think and give our lives
When we hear God give us the call.

T hanking God, we heard him say
     Comes first in all we do
       For He gave us His Son, our Lord,
       For me and also you.
H elping Him by all our deeds
     Can make the world seem good
A sking Him for strength and love
     To serve Him as we should.
N aming Him, our God, our Lord,
     We can tell each one
K nowing Him who loves us all
     Is our task, let's get it done.
S howing friends His love for us
     And also for them too.

Go forth, be brave, tell all the world
Jesus loves me and *you!*

Elizabeth M Sudder

CHILDREN AT THE CHRISTMAS CRIB

See the little Christ child,
      Lying on the straw
Hands outstretched to us in grace,
See His little smiling face!

See His gentle Mother,
Kneeling by His side,
His father Joseph guarding them,
Their faithful friend and guide.

We are happy children,
Full of Christmas glee,
For it is His birthday,
How full of joy are we!

We, the little Christ child see,
On the manger straw,
Already smiles to all in love,
His Holy Family.

There's a little shepherd boy,
      Bringing Him a lamb,
For a little birthday joy,
The very best he can!

Overhead, the shining star,
Led three kings bearing gifts,
Gold and frankincense and myrrh,
Humbly offering Him.

Only some sprigs of holly,
And paper chains we make,
With love He smiles to see them,
We bring for His sweet sake.

Joan Greathead

DYING, WE LIVE!

Do you ever wonder,
When you are alone:
'What's the point of going on,
Now I'm on my own?'

Days seem long and empty
With no-one to share
Meals, or news, or problems,
And no-one to care.

'Does it really matter
If I live, or die?
Living seems so useless
Now there's only I!'

Life is yours to cherish,
Not to throw away;
Soul and body nourish,
Each returning day!

Thank God for the memories
Of the good you've known;
Pray for all the others
Who, too, are alone.

Ask God for the courage
To face each new dawn,
Dying to the old life,
And in faith reborn.

Nancy Solly

GOOD FRIDAY CHORALE

When Jesus was by man divined
In place of dark concealing
We watched with unrelieving mind
All clash of human feeling
Jerusalem and jealousy revealing.

With Peter in the early hours
We found ourselves denying
And, siding with the easy powers,
Cried out for crucifying
Then wished we were the thieves with Him undying.

Alasdair Aston

COLOUR MAN

We are the painter of paintings
Dabbling red, blue and green
Holders of throbbing palettes
Blobbing paint by the reams
We are the canvas stretchers
Undercoat part of the trade.
We ride into day on the sunrise
We lie down to sleep unafraid.
We are the searchers of beauty
We are the placers of bets
Let the sun come in here
As the shadows draw on
Get on and have no regrets.
We all are vain
We all are sane
And will come to the colour man's call.
For the colour man who made the rainbow
Holds the key to it all.

Micaela Beckett

89

CALVARY

Stumbling, He moved on towards Calvary.
Legs aching from the weight of the cross He bore.
Back stinging and stiff from the beating He'd had.
Mind longing to shut out the curses and abuse of the crowd.
Heart thudding within His chest with clutching fear at what was to come,
And love's longing rejected and cast aside.
Too weary, for need of rest, to wipe the spittle
and blood from His aching brow.

'Would I have done all this. Gone through all I did,
Just to say at the end, no I don't think I'll forgive you *that?*
I wasn't playing a game on Calvary.
I wasn't making a show.
I was saying - follow me. All, yes *all* is forgiven.
Follow Me you who are careworn and weary, and I will give you rest.
I will release you from the burdens you are carrying.
But you say *no,* we can manage.
You *want* to carry them alone. *Why?*
Are you stronger than I?
Even I could not carry Calvary alone. Yet you can?
Who are you that you make such claims,
You who spurn the help that I have placed on hand to bless?
You are not what heaven is made of if you spurn Me and those I send to you.
And yet I love you.
My heart bleeds for you.
I long to clutch you to Me and save you from yourselves.
But, I have sworn to give you freedom to choose.
Use it wisely children, use it wisely.'

Christina Fowler

LENT

I sat down to a banquet, but what did I need?
Not my sight - but that which my soul decreed,
To fast on my faults, sins and wrong doing
And to feast humbly with faith, pursuing
All goodness and truth in peace prayer and praise,
Till with love for Christ I'm filled all my days.

Eileen Jackman

I KNOW THAT MY REDEEMER LIVETH

The Gods of earth are void and cold,
No vision here for me to hold;
Yet I a glimpse of Heaven behold
When I gaze on the sacred tree.

My faith is sure when days are bright;
Yet in life's deepest, darkest night
In hope I see the world's true light
Stream from the cross on Calvary.

The cross it is my resting place,
The fountain of redeeming grace;
Through mists I see His dying face,
My Lord and God who died for me.

In life the cross alone can save,
In death, it vanquishes the grave,
My hope of life in Heaven it gave;
By Jesus's mercy, I am free.

Through grace I'll reach the sapphire throne,
Dark Jordan past, life's voyage done,
Adore the Ever-Holy One,
The Crucified who lives for me.

M M L Hadfield

CHRISTMAS

As the year nears its end, and dark winter nights set in,
And the shops have closed their doors - locking their magic within,
The excited chattering of children - heard merrily exchanging
Their demands and longings of the presents Santa was bringing.

Upon the table laid out all aspects of cooking,
Around the plump turkey with stuffing, still steaming,
The Christmas tree lights flashing and tinsel shimmering,
Night draws its curtain - and life lays sleeping.

Silently, swiftly comes the eve of a new beginning -

As a couple try frantically to find a bed for their babe,
In a lowly stable came a boy child, born to save.
Little do we appreciate that special new birth,
As in years to come it would save the whole earth.

For God so loved us and in our sins He could see,
That unless He sent a Saviour our trust in Him could never be,
And in those precious moments as the child drew His first breath,
We could not have realised that in our sins would be His death.

Then night turns to day and the children's glee,
The food, drink and presents there for us all to see,
As excited people in blind merriment be
Forget to say 'Thank you Jesus, for loving me.'

As Christmastide comes and in the height of your pleasure,
Just cast your mind upon God's very special treasure.

His very own Son - *Jesus Christ - Our* Lord.

Margaret A Webb

WHAT IS LIFE?

We are all put on this earth
To perform a different task
I also feel we're duty bound
To try to do as the good Lord asks

From the day we are all born
We know one day we'll die
Trying to do our best for mankind
Before we reach the sky

But! There's so much to be done
As we all tread our daily path
Trying to look to one another
With joy and love not wrath

There are so many lonely people
In this world of ours today
Some of them having heartache
Which will never go away

So if you can give them comfort
Or maybe just lend a hand
Your joy will lift their sadness
Until they reach the promised land

There's a moral to this story!
Try to be loving kind and caring
For this gift the Lord has given you
If you can give you will be sharing.

Lil Walker

GOOD OVER EVIL

Satan, prince of death and sin,
    Tries to devour, and pull you in,
Into his web he tries to entrap,
    And when he can he'll cause mishap.

Satan lover of deceit and lies,
    Thrown down by God from upper skies,
Spreading evil all around,
But through Jesus, goodness we have found.

On the cross, our life's redeemed,
    Jesus spoiled what Satan schemed,
Fear of death He took away,
    That was our Lord's victorious day.

Satan knows he'll never win,
    No matter who He deceives to sin,
God's grace will save them one and all,
    No matter just how far they fall.

With Job He let him have his will,
    But God said, 'Job you shall not kill'
So what really happened on that hour,
    Was God showed Satan - He'd the power.

When the Lord returns, there'll be no more tears,
When He locks up Satan for a thousand years,
When the Lord returns to complete His plan
And brings grace and peace and love to man . . .

Ian T Redmond

DAVID AND GOLIATH

Out there, Goliath struts about,
with mighty sword, he bellows out,
'Who dare fight me, will surely die'
but David, merely wondered, why?

Across the stream, towards the giant,
collecting stones, he looked defiant.
From his tunic, he produced a sling,
this lad, destined to become king.

As he neared the giant's ground,
he examined the stones that he had found,
one was smooth, and shaped quite round,
and Goliath, towards him, began to bound.

Carefully, David loaded his sling,
and to himself, began to sing.
Around his head, the sling he twirled,
and letting go, the stone he hurled.

Goliath, was stopped, right in his tracks,
there amongst his Philistine packs.
Where he fell, the ground was moved,
David's stone, a point had proved.

Giants, and bullies do not matter,
a stone soon ended Goliath's patter.
Brutish strength, will often fail,
and the power of reason, can prevail.

So, for those who feel, they want to fight,
be sure, your cause, is one that's right.
If not, be sure, your time will come,
and to a David, you'll succumb.

Andrew Dickson

I DREAMED

I dreamed I was in heaven amid angels all aglow.
I dreamed I'd left my mum and dad although I love them so.
I dreamed I spoke to Moses, Elijah and Jesus too.
I dreamed I met my grandad, the one I never knew.
I dreamed of where no tears fell, nor grief was there to bear.
I dreamed of people clothed in white with happy party air.
I dreamed of harmony, love and joy outflowing from everyone.
I dreamed of a beautiful land that has no setting sun.
I dreamed of a land untouched by death nor disease its mantle spread.
I dreamed of a place where, in majesty, Jesus was its Head.
I dreamed of perfect peace, permeating everywhere.
I dreamed I lived for ever in this land without a worldly care.
I dreamed of multicoloured birds that sang the sweetest songs.
I dreamed of where right always triumphed for there were no wrongs.
I dreamed, then woke finding frost patterns across my window pane;
Like them, I realised, no two lives are ever quite the same.
Of this life and that yet still to come no comparison can be made.
Yet as I watched the sun's rays creeping rainbow colours spread,
Quite suddenly I knew the love of God right there upon my bed.

Ken Single

THE BLIND MAN

The blind man walked along the road as people rushed about
'I can see him standing there' he heard someone shout
He put his hands against the wall as people pushed along
Then in the distance he could hear the sounds of happy songs

The sun was shining this he knew, the warmth felt on his face
he was safe against the wall, in a sheltered place
Then suddenly the voices seem to come quite near
So he stood there silently no-one would see him here

All at once the voices stop, someone touched his arm
But a gentle voice speaks out 'Please don't feel alarm'
On his eyes he feels a hand, this wipes away his fright
Then as the voice speaks out in prayer, he regains his sight

There are no words that can explain
What this once blind man now feels
To see and touch the hands of Him
Our dear God sends to heal

Dawn Parsons

NEED

Dear Father I need You, I need Your strength,
to help me, now, this minute.
For where I'm going and where I'm at,
there seems no reason in it!
You are my Lord, my Creator, my Guide.
You know what is best for me.
But in my confusion and dark despair,
the way I cannot see.
If I'm meant to feel as I feel right now,
grant me faith to accept my lot.
If mine is the frame, frail though it be,
that bears the burdens that others cannot.
Then help me Lord to cope with it all.
may my wavering spirit be strong.
Help me lay all my cares, my anguish, my hurt,
at Your feet, for that's where they belong.
Strengthen my puny, feeble faith.
Cleanse my heart from all useless dross.
And though blind at this moment I may be.
Keep my eyes fixed firm on the Cross.

Barbara Bradley

FROM THE FATHER, FROM THE SON

Dear Dad,
You knew all about me, even before I was born.
As a child I remember, being held close, quietly in your arms.
When I was a boy, if I had questions,
I'd knock on the study door, seeking your attention.
No matter how busy, you'd spend ages, finding the answers.
Whenever I was hurting, with a bloody nose, or bleeding knee,
You comforted me, and made it better.
You forgave the mistakes of my youth, teaching me,
That wisdom was my sister, and insight my closest companion.
Now as a man, I couldn't ask for a better friend,
I'm still listening, learning and loving you,
Sincerely yours,
A son.

Dear son,
Thanks for the letter,
I was delighted in you from the start, I watched you grow.
I was there whenever you needed me, I dried the tears.
When you stumbled and fell, I picked you up.
Question me, and I would listen, even when saying no.
Sometimes we'd argue, I hated that, but you had to learn.
My son, you are a blessing to me, beyond my best dreams.
You now teach me about life, and I warm to it.
As child, your speech, thinking and feelings, were childish.
Now you've put away childish things, and we meet face to face.
Let's be friends forever.
Keep writing, I love you,
The Father.

Mark Roper

IN YOUR PRESENCE

Lord how can I come into Your presence
Yet the price is paid, the victory won
We need not fear Your awesome majesty
You've cleansed our lives through Your Son
Heirs with Him we stand forgiven
Clothed in righteousness and praise
Adopted sons into Your family
Ever Yours through all our days

Sandra Barton

SEEK THE LORD

Seek the Lord with all of your heart,
Know He is near you and not far apart.
He knows all about you and all of your needs,
He's ready to meet you, so trust and receive.

God is longing to bless you, so reach out in faith;
Take from the Father, just like a child from a plate.
His offer to you is all that you need,
If just like a child you would only receive.

God has many treasures, they lie there in store,
Because of God's children who'll not open the door.
'The door to your heart' He says 'open wide;
I'm longing to bless you, to give and provide.'

God's gift of Himself through Jesus the Son,
The gift of His Spirit for His work to be done.
So seek the Lord with all of your heart
And give Him your all and not just a part.

Janet Allcock

THE GARDEN OF LIFE

When we walk in the garden with Jesus
And quietly commune with Him there.
We can tell Him our worries and troubles
Bring Him our sorrows and care.
He'll listen to us with the loving
That only Jesus can give.
Sharing with us all our problems
If in His presence we live.

It was once in a garden that Jesus
Suffered in anguish and pain.
Praying to His heavenly Father
That He would His courage sustain.
So Jesus knows all about suffering,
Knows how much pain we can bear.
He will give us His help and comfort,
Surround us with His tender care.

Let us walk today in that garden
Where Jesus is waiting there.
Where we may walk and talk with Him
Without a worry and care.
And there in the cool of the evening,
Away from the heat of the day.
He'll listen to us in the garden of life,
And hear us with love while we pray.

Edna Pate

WATER INTO WINE

Great excitement in Cana of Galilee,
Mary and her son Jesus were going there,
To their friends' wedding they'd been invited,
In their happiness they were asked to share.

Tired and hot after walking the dusty road,
They were offered water to bathe their feet,
Then their host brought a very welcome drink,
From an urn, wine, deliciously sweet.

As more guests arrived, more wine was brought,
Everyone wished a good life to the pair,
The urns were emptied one by one,
Of this, the guests were quite unaware.

Then the host, warned by servants of the situation,
Told Mary, 'The wine is nearly all gone;'
She said to the servants 'Do as Jesus tells you,'
She had such great faith in Jesus, her son!

Jesus bade the servants take six stone water pots
And refill them with sparkling clear water,
Then continue to serve this to the guests,
They really wondered whether they ought to!

However, apprehensive, they did as they were bid,
They began to pour, wine, not water, flowed fast!
The guests started to murmur amongst themselves,
'Our host has saved the best wine till last!'

This was the first miracle Jesus wrought
At a wedding in Cana of Galilee,
In what remained of His short earthly life,
Many more wonderful miracles were people to see.

Pat Heppel

A STRANGER

I recognise a stranger
As we walk along the street,
We know of one another
Although we'll never meet.

He may have seen an angel
Or been spoken to by God,
For his soul shines on the outside
And his feet have starlit trod.

His pride has gone forever
And his eyes shine like the dawn;
I recognise a stranger,
A man who was reborn.

Enid Pearson

NOEL

Mince pies and mistletoe,
Ivy and holly,
Candles and Christmas trees,
Santa so jolly.

Carols and pantomimes
Parties so merry,
Chestnuts beside the fire,
Snow on the berries.

Thoughts of the Holy Babe,
Coming in glory,
Peace and goodwill to all,
The same sweet story.

Elsie Pearce

MICHAELMAS DAISIES

'We've waited till the summer heat
And scorching days have passed;
Stood in the background, quietly,
Now may be seen at last.

You're not forgotten; there's a place
And time, to show our flowers,
When evening shadows deeper fall
And shorter, daylight, hours.

Gently, O Christian, raise your eyes
And contemplate the view
When roses fade and lilies fold
There's blessing still for you.

My daisies bloom at Michaelmas,
In harmony their tone,
In contrast to the summer's flowers;
With pastel shades, they come.

Relax, and rest, take time, reflect,
As harvest gifts you store,
Know *He* who gives so generously
Has in His garner, more.

His grace sufficient for the day,
His watchful guard at night,
His constant love Thy armoury,
His blessing, Thy delight.'

St Michael's flowers, I do read
The message that You bring;
The seasons change but *God* remains
My Saviour, Shepherd, King.

Eileen M Darke

SOMEWHERE SOMEHOW

Somewhere somehow,
    I can feel You near.
Somewhere somehow,
    You in me and I in You.

And somewhere somehow,
    in the great *I am.*
You walk beside me,
    Your loving touch will help,
and guide me.

Somewhere somehow,
    time does not stand still.
For You are my creator,
    and I know You are my maker.

Somewhere somehow,
    I give my heart to You.
You fill me with Your Spirit,
    and You make all things new.

Somewhere somehow,
    I just call Your name.
'Jesus come and find me,
    stay with me and walk beside me.'

Somewhere somehow,
    in You I feel secure.
I know that You chose me,
    and I'm Yours forever more.

Somewhere somehow,
    I can feel You near.
Somewhere somehow,
    I know You are there.

Wendy Jackson

HIS MADRIGAL

Their eyes shine, like the light of heaven,
in trusting hope,
the dark, lonely trails, are now
- a distant dream,
He is their friend, their guide.
From war-torn borders -
barriers of hate and vengeance,
once burning brightly,
are moments of the past.
Voices from the skies
travel the air,
minstrels for their brothers.
Crossing western skies,
the madrigals, in African beat,
gather in crescendo unity.
The children's smiles,
echo the peaceful stage
and new found families.
The violent days,
when hurtful paths began,
- are over.
The desert sand blows,
in the almanac of time.
His eyes light the way
and the music
is just beginning.

Annette Jones

LIFE AFTER DEATH

The light is fading all around,
darkness drawing near.
The time has come to say goodbye,
no more pain and fear.
But as the darkness starts to pass,
a brighter light we see,
on into another world,
the Lord has set us free.
For all the memories left behind,
remain deep down inside,
knowing that when our turn comes,
that light will be our guide.
The grief we feel, the sad despair,
of losing someone dear,
will pass in time but still within,
we hold them forever near.

H M Berry

HIDDEN DEPTHS

You are more than your momentary feelings
You have depths that until now are unknown
There are strengths that are hidden deep within you
Wells of courage that are not yours alone.

Built into your Faith are girders of iron
Not seen in the ordinary way
Bedded deep in your spiritual being
Only brought from those depths as you pray.

They give help in those times of confusion
They turn around all your doubts and your fears
Put into perspective the grief and the worries
Turn to smiles the heartbreaking tears.

The Painter in Words

CHRISTUS NATUS EST

Star light, star bright,
Shine out strong and clear tonight.
Guide the ambassadors of the Earth
To a most important birth.
Shepherds up! Be on your way
For this is a holiday.
A King is born, of lineage rare,
In a palace rude and bare.
His courtiers for-legged are,
The royal cradle filled with straw.
Sleep well child, be your slumbers sweet,
Myrrh has no meaning yet awhile.
King of glory, King of light
Bring fresh hope to us tonight.

The carpenter stands near his tools of trade
Looking on with some amaze,
As kings, all dressed in silks and gold,
Bow the knee before his son,
Whilst Mary sits in her homespun,
Smiling her secret tender thoughts.
The shepherds cluster round the door
Looking in with timid awe.
Outside a solitary dog
Sniffs the air and feels fear,
Howls with desolation rare.
At Herod's palace the star's light glistens
On swords being sharpened for their work.

Michael Constant

PEACE ON EARTH

Who was born at Christmas
All men may live again
Let us all remember
When our faith is running low,

Christ is more than just a figure
Wrapped in ethereal glow -
For He came and dwelt among us
And He knows our every need,

And He loves and understands us
And forgives each sinful deed
He was crucified and buried
And rose again in glory

And His promise of salvation
Makes a wondrous Christmas story,
An abiding reassurance
That the little Christ Child birth
Was the beautiful beginning
Of God's plan for Peace on Earth.

Mary Chapman

A SUNDAY MORNING

O why don't they have the service later
Shall I put the alarm clock on
Or chance just to waken
Must remember to take something for the collection

After all it is Sunday morning
And ideas will be forming
For a busy day in the garden
Or maybe with friends, have a party

Yes Lord, I am glad I made it
The bells were ringing, as out I stepped
To reach church as the candles were lit
I entered to find your presence

To receive the bread and wine, this gift so precious
To come and say Thank You, is so small
A thing to do, and to remember
That You died for me O Lord

Kathleen F Dyson

INVISIBLE THREADS

The grief of a man for his wife,
Separated by a thread from this life,
How can you ease the pain?
Only time will provide the strength,
To live the years that remain.

The thread is never broken,
The past is always there,
The happy times, the memories,
The thoughts you cannot share.

The pattern is set, and when the time is right,
Peace will emerge, and show you the light,
The thread that bound you,
Will forever surround you.

Laugh with your heart, be proud that she lived,
Still held by a thread,
For she is within you,
Not far away, and close to your heart.

Anne Roberts

ANOTHER CHRISTMAS

We sit surrounded by plastic holly,
the windows are sprayed snow white.
Half empty bottles tell their secrets,
Christmas descends with all its might.

Safe behind double glazing we watch TV,
our unwelcome doors could not be firmer.
Besieged we shout 'Too early' to night-time callers,
as half forgotten carols die to a murmur.

Four days off work to eat and drink,
to celebrate some ancient birth.
Weighed down with double issue Radio Times,
endless eating, expands my girth.

Faithless promises to go to midnight mass,
wine takes us to sleep at half past ten.
Eating plates piled mountain high,
Queen's speech promises to make us better men.

Can this be all there is to Christmas,
childhood memories of things we've lost?
The shops all have their latest sales,
we buy the bargains - never count the cost.

B Webster

IF ONLY

Where have all the people gone
That were around when you passed away?
Is it they don't want to know
Or they have nothing left to say?

If only they would knock on my door
And say 'How are you today?'
But they are too busy with their lives
To cast a thought my way.

D A White

THE WAY FORWARD

The road won't always be uphill,
though it may seem so now.
Take courage, press on to the top,
you'll find a way somehow.

Dark clouds won't always fill the sky,
lift up your eyes, you'll find
that underneath the darkest one
they're of another kind.

Look for the rainbow, climb the hill,
for here's a different scene . . .
press on and never let despair
take hold, for in between
the hardest times there's always hope
so hold on to the end,
and you will find that hope will be
a very worthwhile friend.

That hill you thought too hard to climb
is conquered when you try,
and you will see blue skies again,
they're not in short supply.

Joyce Higgs

ANOTHER ROAD

If that which you do in life,
is done so without the awareness of love,
then it is better that you stop walking
such a pathway of the physical realm,
and seek another road to harmony
from the books of guidance and wisdom,
that lay with all people within the true 'self'
which all people can reach and come to know,
through the truth of understanding found in faith.

M A Cullen

IT ISN'T FAIR

'It isn't fair,' I cry,
When life seems full of hurt and care
When my dreams are shattered
When the things that matter most to me
All slip away, and in dismay
The empty shell I see.

'It isn't fair?' One questioned,
'Was it fair that I should die
When they hung me high
For things I did not do.
Was it fair, or was it just,
Did I cry out, 'Enough!'
Or did I let them do their worst
That I might do my best for you?'

I turned my head with tears of shame;
I didn't need to ask his name.
'Life isn't fair,' he said.

Paula Worth

LET HAPPINESS SHINE

Oh Lord let us pray that even on the darkest day
Let there be light always in our sight
Don't let our lives be all sorrow and gloom
Let us find love and peace real soon

Please help us to show people we really care
That we always have lots of love to share
In times of need when things go wrong
Help to give us strength and make us strong

Please show us how and help us to pray
Not only at the beginning but at the end of the day
Let happiness shine through for all to see
No matter how hard and cruel life can be

Dorothy R Walker

ETERNAL GRACE

'I am the Way.'
Said Jesus, our brother
'The Father is in Me
And I in the Father.'

'I am the Truth,'
Said Jesus, our friend
'You are My friends
If you keep My commandments.'

'I am the Life,
Sent by the Father
That you might have life
And have it abundantly.'

Alwyn Jolley

WITH THIS RING

*(A prayer composed by a Mother's Union member for the 1450 year
anniversary of Bangor Diocese, North Wales)*

Through centuries past, this House of God
Has nested in surrounding hills,
A hallmark of our Faith.
Within these walls so strong and thick,
Comfort and peace are found by all
Who worship in His name.
Through distant years to modern times
Adoring parents bring their young,
To join God's family.
Now, 'with this ring' they wish to wed,
Two happy souls so much in love,
Present themselves to God.
Bound together by the promise
'To love and cherish, in sickness
And health, till death us part.'
And so the years go stealing by.
The young and old they come and go.
Still God's House stands for all.
As we go on our different ways,
Help us to witness day by day,
Christ's word and truth and love.
Tell how God sacrificed His Son,
To be a shepherd, to mankind,
Such love *will* conquer all.

Patricia Irons

A SUNFLOWER'S SECRET

I stand tall and proud with my head held high,
My face to the sun, smiling up at the sky,
I've reached my target, achieved my goal,
With my height and my beauty I feel in control.

And in the sun's warmth my short life I recall,
My struggle to germinate, sprout, and grow tall,
I was watered and nurtured by a young loving hand,
Then given support so alone I could stand.

I started in life as a tiny seed
In a pot of moist compost, free from all weed,
From a child's gentle hand I was lovingly sown
And because of that love I am now fully grown.

And now in my prime I must think of my end,
Soon my petals will wilt and my stem will bend,
To each busy bee who has been my guest
I thank you for fulfilling my life's request.

You're guessed, I'm a sunflower but soon I will fade,
The Autumn is near and I rest in the shade,
And now for the hand of that sweet child I need
To gently and tenderly extract my seed.

So I shall not mourn as ebbs my tide,
My seeds hold life's secret locked tightly inside,
Out of death comes new life ending grief and despair,
Those small seeds made fertile by God's love and care.

Margaret D Ghori

THE LIGHT OF THE WORLD

Within a rounded arch, a kingly figure stands.
Upon His head a crown of thorns, haloed in light.
White-robed with broidered cloak, falling in gentle folds
O'er sandalled feet. In the silver moonbeam's light
Behind Him, the orchard trees cast shadows in the gloom.
His left hand holds a lighted lantern, high upraised,
Dome-shaped, with lattice panes of varied shape and size,
In which a single candle burns with steady flame.
Three rosy apples lie unheeded on the ground,
Despised and fallen fruits; outside a wooden door
Half hidden by ivy, with briars intertwined.

The white-robed figure is our Saviour blest;
His lamp of Truth, shedding an all revealing light
Spilled out in divers patterns as the Spirit wills;
Shining upon the darkness of our human sight.
The apple orchards, bounteous gifts He would bestow.
The bolted wooden door, a closed and hardened heart,
Within twisted creepers of false desires enclosed;
Obstinately shut to Truth and Light. Patiently He
Stands and knocks, asking admittance of our own free will.

Noelle Wells

BEGINNING AND END

'We came into the world with nothing,
When we leave we will take the same,'
Is a very much quoted saying,
That we've all heard again and again;
But sometimes I find myself wond'ring,
Is it all quite so simple and straight,
Should we take this statement for granted
And accept it as our prescribed fate?

116

'Tis better,' we're told, 'to be giving
Than receiving,' for this shows our love,
But a cheerful giver's a receiver
Of blessings galore from above;
So though we begin life with nothing,
I'm very much tempted to say,
We'll take with us on our final journey
Everything we have given away.

Edward Farren

THE PINK ROSE: A POEM FOR GILL

Each year at this time
My pretty pink rose blooms.

It stands out among the weeds
Reminding me of you.

You stood out among the others,
Before your life was so cruelly cut short.

And though I never need reminding,
Because you are in my thoughts each day,
The rose always serves its purpose:

Your goodness shines through even now -
I cannot grieve any longer,
The sadness has worked itself out,
And a happiness and gladness has taken over -
I'm so *glad* I knew you
I'm so *lucky* to have known you
Your *memory* makes me feel warm and serene

Life goes on
And an inner peace keeps me content.

Beverley Simmons

JESUS WILL NEVER FAIL YOU

I've found a friend who loves me,
A friend, who is faithful and true,
To me, He is all I can ask for.
And He'll be the same to you.

What friend can you discover,
Your sorrows and burdens to share?
There never was found such another
With Jesus you can compare

Your friendship He is needing,
Those loved ones who have gone astray
In sorrow and anguish He's pleading
That they'll find the Narrow Way.

He is the One to guide you
When your life on earth is o'er
Then Jesus will be there beside you
To lead you to Caanan's shore.

Jesus will never fail you,
His promises are true,
He'll never leave you lonely
He'll see you safely through.

When other friends have failed you
And you are left alone,
Jesus will be there waiting
Waiting to take you home.

J H Jarvis

ODE TO CHRISTMAS 1995

Old Christmas comes with ponderous tread,
Diverse traditions here to spread;
Customs old and customs new to weave,
We take up some and others leave;
The transient fads scarce ripple time,
But others are the rocks sublime,
Wrought through decades to our good stead.

First task the mail: posting dates ahead;
That changed address: Is Albert dead?
Some jocular brawl - a mail coach scene;
We can't send that to Mrs Green;
Kith and kin: the right card must be found;
The matching labyrinth unwound;
Jane, did I write to Uncle Fred?

Naked the woods, dormant grass still green;
How low the sun, scarce ever seen;
Dead leaves that hide, in a barren hedge;
Cold black the pool; dead brown the sedge.
Shop windows blaze with luminous delights;
We fight the night with gaudy lights;
Depart you gloom: light up the scene.

Those parties done, cautiously we plod
Our homeward track; stones and icy sod;
With gifts exchanged, rich with food and wine;
The music great: the entertainment fine.
Yet: something more than matter's light,
Illuminates the soul this night;
Gaze upwards at the lamps of God.

Francis E Adams

LOVE SUPREME

If I could look through eyes that see
to behold the beauty that's in store for me
no voice could say no pen could write the
beauty of my loved one.
        If I could shake the stars
from heaven to make a shape or form
for me no rose or flower in fragrance glee
could ever be as sweet as she to me.
        If I could hold that ecstasy and if I see
and touch the stars I see what beauty
there is for me no song is sung in native
sweeter than the harmony with you with me.
        If I could hold the hands divine
in every hour that I find then my time
would not be blind for my true love I have found.
        If minds could think the exact
words to say how different things would
be sincerity holds no stumbling block
and light of knowledge shine forth
and we with our divine creator
        will reign eternally.

E J Sharpe

NIGHT LIGHT

I try to feel Your light in me
But deserve your disapproval
For Jesus only You can see
My sad attempts at stain removal

My tarnished soul is overloaded
With all of life's desires dark
Every sin Your hand has noted
And I can't wash away their mark

God loves a trier, I have heard
Maybe there's hope for me
Although I try, I often fail
My sinning ways set free

Still in the night I call to You
When I feel most alone
And I resolve to follow You
To let your light in me, shine on.

Maureen A Scott

A GUIDING LIGHT

Behold all mortals meek and mild,
Hear ye this night a new born child.
In Bethlehem the stories tell,
Of Jesus, our Emanuel.
And in a manger there he lay,
A guiding light to show the way.
A star so bright that lights the sky,
And angels sing 'Rejoice on high'.
Poor shepherds in the dead of night,
Look up in wonder at the light.
We must make haste, no time to lose,
And follow the star beyond the hills;
And follow it to Bethlehem,
And there to find this place of men.
Fear not for those three shepherds poor,
They came across the stable door.
And peering in this sacred place,
A babe they saw with his grace.
Bowed down their heads in wondrous joy,
And marvelled at this baby boy.

Bernard Smedley

THE OLD MAN

And in his youth
the old man said of many tales,
And now I am old I live in my youth
in my dreams and memories
my mother my father so young my
brothers my sisters playing games running
and jumping with me.
The joys of love so young with my wife
my children my life
and now before the old man finished
he said God stands before me I am so
close I could almost touch upon
upon . . .
The old man was lost to this our earth
and sang songs and tunes of heaven
He said
I go to live in the arms of Jesus
cry out his name
climb upon heaven's clouds and
be forever in His glory
And the old man was not old any more.
And the old man was with angels
and his old age was gone.

Maria Cardona

122

FAITH, HOPE, AND LOVE

Faith is believing, and trusting too!
Hope is the wish, that our dream will come true.
Love is the outcome, the greatest, the best,
Without love, our faith and our hope have no test.

Faith is the depth of our love for the Lord,
Hope sees us through, when all seems discord.
Love binds all three and helps us to live,
When our fellow men need us, we have all to give.

Help us, dear Father, to follow Your way,
Remember Your teachings in every day.
Give us the insight to see others' needs,
Faith, hope and love, and the will to succeed.

Audrey Pincombe

LIFE IS A CIRCLE

Life is a circle - from beginning to end
From the moment we're born our way we must wend.
From baby to child - from child to teenager
Our lives ever changing from minor to major.
How are we using our time here on earth?
Put to good use? Fulfilling our worth?
The circle keeps moving - how long, we don't know
Life is a test, we must give it a 'go'
Do what we can for others - less *me*
Not selfish, more caring - there isn't a fee!
Life is a circle - from beginning to end
We only live once - our ways we must mend!

Mary Buckingham

WHY?

Why is the world like it is today,
With hatred, everywhere?
White man, black man, yellow man too,
Red blood we all do share,
What does it matter,
From which country we do come?
All people are the same,
All the world is one,
Why kill your neighbour?
On his life you have no lease,
Love they neighbour as thyself,
And learn to live in peace,
When peace does reign,
To judgement we will go,
He will not judge the colour of our skin,
Just the goodness we did show.

Kate Brown

GOD'S OUR FATHER

The world is like an open book,
That God has left for us to look,
We make mistakes and don't understand,
But He is there with open hands,
To reassure us when we're lost,
He loves us at no extra cost,
As children we all learn,
As parents we show concern,
God our Father up above,
We, Your children need Your love.

Simone Blewer

PASSING YEARS

Childhood, girlhood, young womanhood,
All past as in a dream.
Marriage, children all are grown
How short the years now seem.
How swiftly this life passes by!
How imminent looms eternity!

I praise the name of Jesus
That His saving grace I know.
So I need feel no fear or dread
As the years so swiftly go.
For they bear me nearer to Him I love,
To my place in the Father's house above.

My friend, this faith to you I commend
As you travel along life's road.
For Jesus can add to all our joys,
And lighten the heaviest load.
And, at last, when the journey is complete,
We'll meet again at His piercèd feet.

Anne Workman

CREATOR

Sensitive mind, spiritual sign
Sheltered spirit gains flight
Discovers the valve of life
When past, one shines like gold
Rewards, appearance hardly grows old
Remains child-like
While butterflies visit at night.

Alan Jones

ALL THINGS WORKING FOR OUR GOOD

When your hopes are dying
        For a thousand things you've tried
Not one of them successful
        You've just sat down and cried

The bible brings you this message
        And I know you'll prove it true
God will make things work together
        Just for the good of you

The man who thus encourages us
        Was an example to us all
If any man knew suffering
        It was the apostle Paul

They shut him up in prison
        So no longer could he preach
Yet still through his epistles
        God's Word he could ably teach

By putting pen to paper
        Though his voice could not be heard
He reached a larger audience
        We can still read every word

So, did things work together
        For good? Oh yes, it's true
Men couldn't stop God's blessing
        Whatever they tried to do

So many things have happened
        That we've not understood
But I know if we love Him
        He'll use them for our good

Harold Kemp

THE END OR THE BEGINNING?

She really looked so peaceful
Lying there . . as if in sleep,
Slipping slowly away now
I tried not to weep.

Having suffered for many months now
So this was her final release,
No more hurt or painful treatments
At last . . . she was at peace.

The moments ticked by so slowly
It was traumatic . . . I held my breath . .
It was a special occasion
The exact time of my Mother's death.

I felt very emotional
Thanked God that I was there,
So I could hold her for the last time
As I bowed my head in prayer.

I recalled her long and fruitful life
She was nearly ninety one,
And had spent her life caring for others
But now her life on earth was done.

She was going to her just reward
Not just leaving the family
God would take care of her now
Through all eternity.

Mary Anne Scott

ONE PERSON

Why is one person better-looking than any
          other person,
and why is one person nicer to get on with
          than any other person,
why does one person make you more happy than
          any other person
and why does one person make you feel more special
          than any other person could,
why is one person so beautiful, so loving, so adoring
          and such a babe
        why is this one person mine?
        why are you this one person?

D J Nelson

TEARS
(Written in hospital two days into my first experience of motherhood)

Tears of joy
At your birth
Tears of fright
At the responsibility
Tears of bewilderment
As you cry too
Tears of panic
You look so small
Tears of wonder
At your perfection
Tears of thankfulness
For the privilege
Tears of sadness?
Not at this demanding little blessing!

C E Holwell

THE REALITY OF FAITH

Faith, hope and love,
These three abide.
Those who love have hope,
When we are born.

They show their faith,
By prayer and action,
In their infant's care,
And so we grow in strength.

People of prayer and action
Become the strongest in the world,
Seeking how best to serve,
The God of love in all mankind.

Each of us turn towards Him,
As beliefs of childhood,
Taught with loving care,
Grow upwards into faith.

God has no grandchildren;
Each of us respond to Him,
Uniquely as His child,
Strengthened to face the world.

We stand within the world,
Kept steadfast by His grace,
Knowing we are called,
To serve the human race.

In the fullness of Life's circle,
We give grace to others,
Thereby growing into God,
The mystic source of all creation.

D Abell Wood

OUR FATHER IS ETERNAL

The sparkling crystal blanket covers all in purest white,
The imperfections of the earth now hidden from our sight.
A scene so lovely to behold, transformed before our eyes,
But let it not deceive you, this is just a guise.
For thaw will come most certainly and faults will be unveiled,
They cannot be forever masked - the camouflage has failed.

Can there be surer way of blotting out our sin,
A permanent and lasting cure that cleanses from within?
A cover that will never cease our failings to defend,
That time will not erase, and death is not the end.

Yes, long ago in stable bare, of poor and humble birth,
The blessed Son of God was born, Saviour of the earth.
The angels sang His praises then and shepherds bowed the knee,
It was their privilege and joy the infant king to see.

And now today, it was for us, this holy babe was born,
For us He died and rose again on that first Easter morn.
Our Father is eternal, not temporary as snow,
His love will keep us ever as in His grace we grow.
Remember now the infant Christ amidst the festive mirth,
For can we have salvation without the virgin birth?

Lynda Chick

LIFE!

It's not what we have or hope to achieve,
It's having the faith in what *you* believe.
Doing the things that to you seem right
Will give you a character that shines like a light.

Seek peace my friend and if you can,
You will be the quiet man
Who goes through life and gets things done
From early dawn till setting sun.

When you look back on life and what you have done,
It seems so trivial to the achievements of some.
But in some small way you have earned your rest,
If you know in your heart you gave of your best.

Life's travel we know is tinged with despair,
But who on earth is paying the fare?
For on we must go until we come to an end,
But my ambition is meeting my *friend.*

Alan Bellamy

THOUGHT OF THE DAY

Sometimes life is hard, the daily routine we have to
subject ourselves to
But there is that old saying, that there is always
someone worse off than you.
I was at the train station and I saw this young girl
pretty but unkempt
I bet that after leaving school this wasn't the life
that she had dreamt.
There she was stubbing out a fag
Lying in hopelessness with all her worldly possessions
in a filthy sleeping bag.
I thought look at this young girl she should be enjoying
the joys
Of doing her exams, partying, discovering boys.
Soon she will slowly slide slowly sink
Into the dangerous temptations of drugs and drink.
My mind just thought as I became profound
What's a pretty girl like you doing begging at
London Underground?

Gary Gibbs

LIVE

What is this life when we just stand and stare
'Stand and stare' yet know there's no-one there?
No-one there to help us on our way,
To get us home to face another day.

When we grow old some days are full of woe,
We're old - alone - and have no place to go;
Your friends grow old, and sometimes we feel ill,
So what is life but hours we have to fill?

If you feel sorry for your lonely state
There is no need to blame it all on *fate*;
The world is full of folk who're lonely too
So why decide that *fate* has picked on you?

When we are old we think of days gone by,
And can remember times when joy was high.
We *should* recall those days so full of love,
When we felt blessed by someone up above.

There is no need to sit around and mope
For life is good, and still so full of hope.
Feel confident - no matter what your age,
Decide today you start a fresh, new page.

Those days of old have disappeared, it's true,
But up above the sky is still as blue;
The sun is warm and though the rain is wet
We can still feel . . and know we're not dead yet.

You'll know life still has many things to give,
And years don't matter when you want to live.
Live each day as if it were your last
And you'll not care how many years have passed.

Elizabeth Tanner

FULL MOON

The sky is clear
The moon is bright
The night is light
The light is soft
The air is cool

The grass is damp
The stars are scarce
The moon is round

The moon mountains stand clear
The craters marked out
The moon holds sway
With the turn of the tides
As it ebbs and flows

The moon works like clockwork
Predictable certain and sure
Not faltering
Or stumbling along
Smoothly in orbit
Travelling around

A world that is shining
And hiding the moon
Waxing and waning
Rising and falling
Reflecting its light
For you and for me
Never changing
But giving again and again

A V R Cracknell

FOR ALL THOSE WHO SUFFERED AT ST LUKE'S

My condolences and prayers
Go to all who suffered
To the children, and people of Blakeney
For innocent kids, just enjoying themselves
'Tis a nightmare, not a bad dream
'Oh Lord' in Your mercy
Look down upon them
And give them the courage they need
Help them to forget
Please help them to be strong
And as life goes by
Help them to forgive
The one who did them wrong
There's a reason for everything
As we all know
Only God knows,
What or when
For all they have suffered
Please God,
Let it not happen again.

Sheila Wall

THE GIFT OF LIFE

Now I bow my head and pray,
For the glory of the day,
That I go to meet with You,
It's really what I want to do.

Though some days are long I fear,
Deep inside I feel You near,
This makes everything quite clear
Lord I love You very dear.

Because I know You died for me,
On a wooden cross in Calvary,
The reason? It's quite plain You see,
So we can reach eternity.

And the pain You suffered there,
There is nothing to compare,
So I humbly say to You
Thank You for Your gift to me.
                    Amen.

Karen Thompson

TEARS

Lord, take away these tears
For I do not know from whence they came.
Was I touched by hand or did you
reach down to me?
Did I hear a voice so tender that
tears were my only release?

Are they the tears that come from
realisation of the
love and joy we stand amid?

Lord, we know how a word said can
bring tears and yet was
meant to be a tender heart filled
joyous moment of love.

Lord, let my tears come from my
heart, help me to make them
a thing of joy while I stand among
the wonders of nature, showing that
a tear is not just for sorrow or pain.

Donald Dullaert

WILLIAM, OUR FRIEND

William you and I, we had an understanding,
a true friendship that was never demanding.

Together we had laughs and guffaws . . . you always told a good joke
and to all our friends and colleagues, you were a truly likeable bloke.

You were always there to help another in their hour of need,
your motto each day was always to give to others and do a good deed.

What goes around, comes around, is what you would have said,
for life is here for us all to receive, too late when we're dead.

Noticing in a newspaper, I saw with awesome regret,
the horrific news about you in the Evening Gazette.

William, finding it so difficult to believe, I continued to read,
that life had been so cruel to you . . . and you'd had to leave.

When you'd had despairing anguish of your own,
you'd never asked for help . . . you'd just stayed at home.

But you were always there to help another in their despair,
so, where were these people for you . . . did they not care?

I shudder trying to think what had made your life so bad,
and the total despondency you must have thought you'd had.

The priest said that you had travelled to a much better place,
with no more arguments, disputes or ugly scenes for you to face.

As I'd stood during the service staring up towards the church ceiling,
I felt I'd let you down, ... and still not really truly believing.

The coffin that had lain before us all shining and made of oak,
hadn't really been yours . . . just all a distasteful joke.

I simply couldn't believe it had been you . . . your body inside,
it was hard to accept, that you, that loving jolly man had really died.

As you were so special, I wish more than anything for you that day,
that your circle of life could have persuaded and authorised you to stay.

Because from this world, . . . thirty eight is no age to leave,
conscientiously your entity in heaven, will continue, I believe.

Heather Sephton-Taylor

THE EVIL EYE

Leaving the insolent waiter,
I the shadow among men
drift through the dark/green
tinged canyons of streets to the
stadium.
'Give us Barabbas!'
screams the crowd, the
breweries' motley crew.
Even the Greek/Cypriot has
the heart of a statue.
The clouds filter red/black,
there is a pulsing in the sky.
Let them call their taverns
'The Dogs' for they have gone
to the dogs long ago.
The population stands before the
forlorn figure like dumb masochists.

Hear that noise like snake/cobras
cracking jokes to one another?

The Horde is coming!
Black/moon millions.
Beware the Evil Eye!
Beware I.

Thomas E Murphy

EMPTY ARMS

Tiny, perfect, lifeless baby boy,
There lay my firstborn son.
I struggled to cuddle him for the first and last time
Amidst a haze of drugs, grief and unbelief.

Paul Matthew was his name, a 'little gift of God',
Although he was so small, he was perfectly formed,
And I examined his every part
Wondering why this had to happen to me.

Sister said it was time to say goodbye,
So she took him away in his little cot,
And I was left alone . . . with empty arms
And a broken heart.

And yet . . . somewhere in the deep recesses of my soul,
A sense of privilege rose,
For God had allowed just a tiny glimpse
Of what it must have meant for Him
To give up His lovely Son to die for me.

And now . . . I can tell you that ten years on,
My God heals hearts and binds up wounds,
For He has filled my empty arms with two lovely little girls.
And mended my broken heart, the pain has gone.
Thank You Lord!

Dawn Armstrong

BAPTISMAL PROMISES

Around the font proud parents stand
With vows on lips: this holy ground
Has welcomed many through its doors
To valiantly fight for Jesus' cause
Godparents' promises fade like the day
As the candle is snuffed that lit the way
A photo or video of family dressed
In all of their finery, their real Sunday best
Is the only reminder of that special day
When God invited them all to stay
So many are brought through tradition and right
How many return? How many lose sight
Of the family of God with arms opened wide
Like the man on the cross who for all of us died?

Heather Walker

PSALM 50

There are many things for which I need Your mercy.
Things from long ago not yet resolved in me -
Scars of past years.
Things I cling to for fear of losing them -
Though I know them to be transient.
Things which are sometimes hard to forgive -
Though a requisite to the forgiveness I need from You.
Pour on me Your grace - as the waters of baptism.
And now, cleansed from sin
I render You thanks and praise -
And witness to Your glory.

Anne Donockley

MASTERS OF THE AIR
(On the occasion of seeing swifts in flight over Victoria Road)

A living canopy over my homeward path
    Glistening shadows of shapely form
        Silhouettes in a cloudless sky

Lithe spirits of summer grace
    No winter cold hath e'er caught thee
        O bird of warmth and space

Inside my room by dawn by dusk you
    briefly peep in upward flight intent
A thousand thanks for sheer delight
    Near-far ephemeral sprite

Exquisite happening ear and eye quickening
    Wheeling, squealing, sweeping, swooping
        Smooth breath-taking flight
    Parting, darting, gliding, flying
        Patterns of intricate delight

Swiftly-winging now high now low
    Catching angelic whisperings
        Pulsing a path from heaven to earth
        In one
            Eternal
                Now

Joan McCagney

IN THE BLEAK MID-FUTURE

I look into the future
through the chasms of my mind,
but find that there is no happiness
in the numerous things I find.

Kaleidoscopic colours rotate among each scene
causing mass distortion
of what will be
and what has been.

But in the chaos of these things
the future looks quite bleak,
friends are very thin on the ground
and all are afraid to speak.

It seems that the world goes from bad to worse
with love and friendship dying out,
the future looks filled with hatred and violence
so what is it all about?

So many people unemployed
the young have nothing to do,
taking drugs and cursing
even sniffing glue.

And yet life never was like this
people were thoughtful and kind,
it seems that moving with the times
has affected the once innocent mind.

They say we must move with the times
and life cannot stand still,
but what is the point of moving with the times
where people only steal and kill.

Victor R A Day

BATTLE DONE

Waiting.
'Who is?'
I am.
Did an angel not sigh
in the cold night sky?
'Perhaps -
but see the night's long star' -
Listen -
can you not hear
the crystal sea . . . ?
'Perhaps.
But I see the silver moon' -
Waiting;
'What for?'
Waiting to open
Heaven's door
and
to see the things
I hear.

Ray Nurse

FAMILY LOVE

There's an emptiness inside me,
It seems I cannot fill.
Memories alone are not enough,
My sadness lingers still.

My loved ones gather round me,
Concern e'er in their eyes.
Trying to help me to forget the pain,
I seem unable to disguise.

They know that they are dear to me,
They too, a love have lost,
Who shared their joys and sorrows.
Irrespective of the cost.

I appreciate their love for me,
And the void they try to fill.
Whilst they may walk along with me,
They cannot climb my hill.

Harry M M Walker

FOREVER FRIEND

Remember all the lonely ones
each night and day in prayer.
God's presence then they may feel
such love and strength to share.

A ray of light to show the way
to know the Lord is there.
Give them peace within their hearts
much tenderness and care.

Forever friend to one and all
Jesus is by our side
list'ning always each long hour
our Father, teacher, guide.

Time to give to everyone
His arms are open wide.
Never to be alone again
in Him we can confide.

Margaret Jackson

A NEW LIFE

Peaceful in mind and soul
Away from stresses and strife,
My being, now feeling whole
The start of a new life.

Looking at life at a different angle
Trying to see things so differently,
Twisted thoughts that were all in
A tangle
Now able to think clearly.

Learning to enjoy the simplest of
Things
Making the most of each day,
And knowing that whatever life brings
Is to make the most of it in every
Way.

J Bell

IT'S ALL IN MY MIND

What a beautiful mind I must have, when all day and night long, my mind is on my God. The God of my heart, the God in my mind and soul, who gave me His spirit who tells me in my heart to do beautiful things, to do them for Him, He tells me in my mind to love everyone to please Him, I give my mind, heart, and soul to my God. The God who gave me His beautiful love to love each other, and put it in my mind and in my heart, He gave me His spirit never to part as long as I live, the God of my heart, will never leave my mind because the God of my love is all in my mind never to part. It's all in my mind, the grace of love from my God, and what a beautiful gift He has graced me with, from the God of my heart, He's always on my mind, never to part, it's all in my mind. The spirit of love never to part.

Margaret Bush

144

CHILDREN

Has the world gone mad?
Do we count the cost
Of changing what is right
Half the world is starving
The other says 'I want
Children.'

Do you have the courage
To care for eighteen years
For someone who depends on you
Each hour, each day, each year?

It isn't just the glamour
Of pretty pink and blue
It's time, it's love
It's putting them
Before all things. And you.

But still the scientists practise
To alter what should be
A child, created just by love
As is the natural way

Such love embraces all the world
Of children, black or white
Give them a home if left alone
Your life will be fulfilled.

Eunice Birch

MY DEAR CHILD

Do you not realise, how My Heart breaks, when you won't accept the fact that I truly love you, that you are far more precious to me, that the brightest jewel could ever be?
Why do you turn away from Me, to search for comfort amidst other sources?
Have I ever let you down, during your moments of deep distress. Either by bereavement, unemployment or other trials?
Isn't it Me, who hears all who call to Me for help?
Even when hope seems to have permanently vanished, and friends forsake you!
Are you not aware, that the suffering of all My children, deeply grieves Me?
Remember, I will always be close at hand, even where you'd least expect to find Me!
Whether it be amongst prisoners, drunkards, gamblers, the mentally sick, or those souls who are simply lonely.
Wherever the need is greatest for My Love and Compassion, that's where you'll find Me! All I ask, apart from your sincere repentance to turn away from all things evil - is, just to have complete faith in Me!
I never promised, you'd walk as if through a rose-garden, as you tread this earth.
The Way, will often be as steep and craggy as the highest mountain.
But, if you are prepared to follow My footsteps, I'll remain with you through all eternity.
Always,
Your very loving
Heavenly Father
God bless you!

Muriel A Ross

AN IRISH QUESTION

What is buried in this heart of mine
that struggles for my place of birth?
Some planetary pull, my starry sign
imprinting codes of heavy worth?

History full of things long gone to rest
upon the soil of this small isle,
imbuing it with dread, passion dressed,
to surface now in surges wild.

Inheritance, an island filled with strife,
blood stained soil cried out for more,
draining Celtic children dry of life.
What is burning in my core?

Is it earthy soil, or power I crave,
kill and maim by fellow man?
Is it sentiment, arising brave,
to flames my feelings like a fan?

If I could probe the deepest depth and find,
bring to light its vital source,
find this damaged gene of humankind,
isolate this primal force.

Imprint it deep with peace and active power
to stop this hurt of man and earth.
Conceive a seed immune to crass desire,
so future children come to birth.

Only 'The Creator' knows the code
to rectify this strife within,
hate, that hungers in my heart for blood.
In seeking Him will Ireland win?

Joan Bradley

A PART TO PLAY

They say all the world's a stage.
And our roles are determined at an early age.
Well for me some-one had a plan.
To play the part of a foolish man.
For this I didn't have to audition.
They say I'm a fool with no competition.
But even though I play the fool
He uses me as a tool.
He's given me a part to play in life.
Helping me through the trouble and strife
He's also my confidant and friend.
With someone I don't have to pretend
He's there when things go wrong.
He builds me up and makes me strong.
Even when I play the fool and act the clown
He never seems to let me down.
Who is this person, I hear you say.
Who is the one that shows me the way.
I'm talking of my friend Jesus
Who died on the cross to release us.

Paul Adlam

MY LORD

My Lord is my life
my Lord is my love
He helps me in strife
to divine His will above

Jesus, O Lord You gave me Your grace
the ability to see Your heavenly face
You cradled me in Your arms
and kissed me full of life

I loved You from afar
but You drew near
like an eternal star
You blew away my fear

I trusted Your will, You gave me my fill
I showed mercy, You let me win
I am Your servant, but You made Your friend
You promoted me up, I am loyal to the end.

Christopher P Gillham

JESUS CHRIST OUR SAVIOUR

I was lost, you found me.
I was blind, I saw your Light.
I was dead, you raised me,
I was lonely, you visited me.
I had no dreams, you gave me hope.
No-one cared, you gave your life.
I was speechless, you gave me tongues of fire.
My brokenness, you healed.
I had no reason to live, now I live for you.
My love was worthless, you replaced it with yours
I was deaf, you gave me a sign.
Now I hear you speak.
My heart was hard as stone, you replaced it with yours.
My bitterness, you changed into joy.
My sadness, you poured the oil of gladness over me.
I was lifeless, you gave me a garment of praise,
Now I worship you, with thanks giving in my heart.
My mind was in torment and fear.
You gave me a spirit of power, love, and a sound mind.
Born again am I.
I live for *Jesus, praise the Lord.*
Thank our heavenly Father for His precious Son,
Jesus Christ our Saviour Amen.

Grace Seeley

RAINBOW PROMISES AFTER STORMS

Through adversity, keep believing,
Tomorrow's black clouds will be leaving.
As shadows fall, rise up, reach sun's day,
Tread one step at a time, walk life's way.

Try forgiving wrongs seven times seven
To earn love lasting peace in heaven.
Turn again cut cheeks for oppressors.
Learning, wisdom - hard life's confessors.

Keep weeping eyes looking at hope's stars.
Have faith beyond earth, reach for Mars.
Summer suns will shine on better days.
Past hurts will fade into misty haze.

Lose true ways, bitten by serpent schemes;
Never give up hope on heart-held dreams.
Grasp life's banisters, hold God's stairway
Heart tears will return to smiles some day.

Happier times follow pain, end strife,
You will survive tough challenges in life.
Take heart, achieve your special dream.
Though rough journeys are not all they seem.

Little by little, you really can,
An individual, unique rib man,
Overcome difficult rocky roads
Believe in yourself! Evil erodes.

Beyond horizons, rainbow promises,
Paint colour over darkest demises.
Time shadows hurt with every dawn.
Renew faith, live, feel glad to be born.

Look for love's goodness. Follow your heart.
Life's privilege makes grey clouds depart.

Hilary Ann Morris

GOD'S LOVE

I am disabled and that's a fact
but God can use me even in that

Sometimes I am tired and sad
Jesus steps in and makes me glad

When my limbs are stiff and sore
Jesus comes and gives me strength the more

When my mind is in a spin
Jesus gives me victory to win

When I am weak Thou art strong
Jesus puts within my heart a song

When I am down and in doubt
Jesus makes my heart to shout

When my heart is full of sin
Then Jesus brings His peace within

When I cannot say how I feel
Jesus comes down and makes Himself real

When in a panic I run to You
You give me Your love to see me through

Yes I am disabled that is true
But I still desire to work for You

Now I want to thank You for Your love and
Your strength that brought me through

Now I am ready to give my all
Because You are my Lord of all

When all I feel like is giving up
You give me the strength to look up

Ann Bradley

LIFE

Life is like a river
Flowing on and on
Sometimes feeling wonderful
And sometimes put upon

All rivers will have stones
That are steps upon the way
These are a blessing
As our Good Lord would say

Stones to cross the River
The River of Life I'm sure
As each new day opens
Another brand new door

Friends are like the stepping stones
To give help along the way
Who can say what size we'll be
Only the Lord can say

We thank Him, be it pebble
Or boulder, in the flow
Whether giving or receiving help
Onward stepping stones go

Onward and onward
The River of Life doth flow
Help is all around you
Trust the Lord to know

Sylvia Chandler

HUMILITY

The Disciples they to Jesus came
With many a difficult question
Jesus He would then explain
With a simple illustration
You called us Lord, to work with You
Please tell us, make it clear
Which one of us will greater be
When in Your kingdom we appear

Will it be Peter, James or John
Give us the revelation
Will You choose him? Or maybe me?
I'm such a special person.
You bade us Lord, come follow You
And quickly we did come
Now tell us Lord Your point of view
Such great things *we* have done

Jesus He could answer not
This question of the proud
He turned, He looked and then He called
A small child from the crowd
He set him in the midst of them
'Take note of what you see
You must become as this small child
Be humble just like Me.'

Barbara Howard

RETURN TO EDEN

Like heaven descended, Eden shone,
Glorification of angels caressed the morn,
Reverence abundant, across mountains echoed,
Glowing sun rays bestowed warmth,
In unison with God, all nature rejoiced.

Like a lion ferocious, Lucifer portrayed his displeasure,
Cast out of heaven, his intent apparent,
To disrupt such angelic euphoria,
Amid the creation of Adam and Eve,
Satan planned his vengeance.

A garden bestowed through love,
Rescinded despondently beyond recall.
Thus, began amid unforeseen heartache,
Man's initial slaying of his fellow man,
The first callous and futile steps,
Unto eventual and inevitable destruction.

Six thousand years the Creator has awaited repentance of man,
Wars raged like uncontrollable tempests,
Across the elapsing century's misapprehensive cloak.
And now the twentieth century hovers ominous.

The loyal Christian saints await the redemption promised,
Wars and rumours of wars foretell our distance from paradise.
Yet, amid carnage and hope apparent,
Shall appear at last, our return to Eden.

S Kettlewell

WANDERERS RETURNED

The birds they came and went
All day in labour spent
A nest they came to prepare
For their little ones to share

We watched them come and go
And what joy to be part of this show
Each with beak full of twigs
To make a nest for their chicks

The second year they came
Mr Blue-Tit wearing a ring with his name
Very conscious were the pair
Knowing eyes were looking everywhere

As days went by we saw the little ones appear
Waiting for Mum and Dad to draw near
Very cautiously they came with eyes alert
Not wanting their young to be hurt

As time went by
We knew the little ones soon would fly
One morning heads came out to look around
We stood not making a sound

Gradually confidence was gained
As feet steadied and were sustained
Away they flew one by one
We hope next year back they'll come.

Hannah Webber

A LITTLE WAITING

The waiting for an unknown day,
The waiting when in work and play,
The waiting shivering all alone,
　　　The waiting cold and quite unknown.
What is life to play us so?
What is death that bids us go?

The waiting on this crater abyss,
The waiting for its shattering slip,
The waiting to float, arms outstretched,
　　　The waiting to smell the itch of pitch.
What is life to play us so?
What is death that bids us go?

The waiting for what we are,
The waiting expedience near or far,
The waiting to see that dazzling light,
　　　The waiting in agony of delight.
What is life to play us so?
What is death that bids us go?

L Brown

FOR MOTHER

What pains a mother gladly gives
to keep her child in safety's cradle
from bosom held enduring change
nurtures every step and fall.

A love unfettered always shown
behind the smile, the sigh, the wish
that nothing change this perfect love
between the innocence of both.

Does memory of that babe not bring
some flash of longing when she's grown,
to hold her in your arms again
and feel that gentle trust of love?

Although the years have changed us both
this woman is still the child you held,
the bond, the trust, the need is still there
for mother your daughter loves you.

Helen Saunders

BATTLEFIELD BROTHERS

War torn cities in civil war
With missiles, blown-up buildings.
Widowed, orphaned, what's it for?
What are these people gaining?

Yesterday were brothers
Walking side by side,
Now fighting 'gainst each other
Their sight they can't abide.

Who'll stop this senseless killing,
Maiming, and the hate?
Learn to live together,
Before it's all too late.

Innocent people dying,
People too young to die.
But can you really hate them
When you look them in the eye?

Simon Martin

ALL GOD'S CHILDREN

Temper justice with compassion,
But for the grace of God go I,
Or you, if you had starving children,
Would you allow your child to die?

We are all God's children, set down upon this globe.
The poorer nations hungry, in their huts of clay adobe.
We buy the crops from poorer nations and leave them without bread.
Whilst we in richer nations are well housed and so well fed.

What should we do to help, we say;
We must pray to God to show us the way;
A way to share earth's riches we must find,
And bring equality to all mankind.

Jean M Senior

THE MAN AND THE TREE

The tree stood tall, strong and splayed
And from it a cross was about to be made
The tree did not like it and started to cry
Because it knew that a man was going to die
The man watched the tree, and saw how it cried
He said 'No more crosses from you shall be plied'
From then on the tree has been slender and fine
With delicate branches where flowers entwine
In each flower centre, broken stamens form a ring
A replica of the thorns. That once crowned a King
All the petal edges are tipped with red
A reminder of the wounds that hurt and bled
'Christ' was the man so unjustly condemned
The cross a cruel support to his body did lend
He died on 'Good Friday' dark day of mystery
A crucifixion and the transformation of a tree.

Margaret Cottam

CONTEMPORARY CHRISTIANITY

The cynics today, say that virtue doesn't pay,
the common consensus of secularity;
but our church congregations continue to pray . . .
Kyrie eleison, Christe eleison.

Most contemporary Christians take some stick
from some atheists, socialists and heretics;
but ancient Gregorian chants sound majestic . . .
Gloria in excelsis Deo.

The gospel according to grim, agnostic wits
is that churchgoing Christians are hypocrites;
but faith remains the inspiration of poets . . .
Credo in unum Deum.

Nowadays we hear theories like evolution,
Christian scientists may have the solution;
Gene-sis may start a counter-revolution . . .
Sanctus, sanctus, sanctus.

How do churchmen justify Christianity?
It's a mystic exit from gross inanity,
the rejection of false creeds, pride and vanity . . .
Pater noster, qui es in coelis.

What is the *raison d'être* of Christianity?
To achieve salvation and the soul's sanctity,
that normally means quality not quantity . . .
Agnus Dei, qui tollis peccata mundi.

What's religion's influence on society?
To raise morals and our sense of propriety,
and inspire much piety and charity . . .
Confiteor, Deo omnipotenti.

Louis Brophy

FATHERS' PRIDE SONS DERIDE

Father says proudly that's my big son
Not why he ran and left Mom.
He didn't left us a bun
Instead he shot off like a gun
Was it that he'd had his fun? And see
His responsibility as a pun
My conception, the evolution of the race
Why should it be made into a disgrace?
As it sure did when Father raced away
From my mom.
Strange it is, but fathers stood their grounds
Less someone elses' moms would found
They sure do tread on holy grounds
But then disappear like careless hound
Pity Dad you didn't bide your pace and
Helped dear Mom through my growing phase
If only till my weaning years
So I could now your praises raise
Father! Remorse is making you shake
Beads of sweat are cascading down your face
I know you feel it was a waste that my
Childhood dreams you did not taste
But phases like these don't hesitate
That's why you should have cooperate
Instead of finding yourself in this sad state
Still no bitterness will I accommodate
I know some, true fatherhood mistake,
And their burdens unto moms do shake.
I now fatherhood anticipate, and shall
Wholeheartedly participate in, moulding and
Nurturing my son and then I would have won
The true joy of fathering my son, true fatherhood.

Glen-Ciel Campbell

ON PASSING THE PARK

The night is cold, the sky is dark,
As I wander home past Fishponds Park.
The sounds of lovers kissing there -
Hangs like a fragrance in the air.
Such sweet romance, alas, it seems
That I to bed must dream my dreams.
Such happy memories I recall,
When we were young and did it all.
I stop, I listen, and ask, 'Oh when -
Will my love and I do that again?'

The stars are shining in heaven bright,
As I to bed and say, 'Good night.'
For I am here, and so alone,
Whilst my love sleeps so warm at home.
My heart is broken, my spirit sad,
I've thrown away all that I had.
A girl that loved me in my youth,
Has left me here to face the truth.
I can take no more, I've had enough -
Whatever has happened to our love?

A love that's known near thirty years,
Has ended up now all in tears.
Let's work together, put it right,
So once more we may say 'Good night.'
And hold each other once again,
I'll wipe your tears, you ease my pain.
The lovers part, they go their way,
Tomorrow is another day,
When they can meet just after dark -
And steal a kiss in Fishponds Park.

S Johnson

LIGHT POEM

Clear light
Lead me
From the dark side
Of the night
To the centre
Of my sight
Where a small light
Echoes the divine . . .

Anna Meryt

A LITTLE PRAYER

Dear Jesus our light of light,
Hear us in humble prayer,
Be with us on our daily round,
Help us other's burdens to share.

Let your light upon us shine,
Your mercy on us bestow,
That we may with faith sublime,
Your love forever know.

When the busy world is hushed,
When day-light fades away,
Dear Jesus grant us Peace serene,
Should 'Restless Night' hold sway.

And, in the morn if skies be grey,
Help us to be cheerful in all we do,
Forgetting all the snares we meet,
And trusting only You.

Daisie Cecil-Clarke

ECLIPSE

Dwarf hides - covered by billowing skirts
of enormous shadow;
brightness played a game - it poured light and
Truth straight upon their forms.
What hell of noise and shouting! Stirring,
in bog of stagnation;
stinking smell; this is *the* place for me!
Light goes out to pray. Dwarf
and shadow pant in relief; so close!

Enormous shadow holds dwarf tight. 'Game
was unfair - light was strong -
light must be kept dim - it's as if we're
formless heaps!' Shadow holds
out its mass-less being to protect
dwarf. Dwarf slips through floppy
ease, stopping shadow shrinking. Tired
shadow wakes up to find dwarf gone. The
game is remembered. Dark

shadow whimpers - fears light may catch dwarf;
may realise piercing
brightness will understand, nurture, free.
Shadow shakes itself to
stretch formless self - makes noises to
become big. Yet light holds
dwarf clear from becoming caught by dark
shadows over the earth.
The dwarf, freed, is an erupting rock!

Shadow has lost its hold; creator
multiplies light, formless void, void! Word
was, is. Light shines. Rock holds fast; God breathes.

Robert Shooter

163

FOLLOW THE PATH

Let the angels bless
One like you with
A kiss so very holy
Feel the goodness in
A heart like yours
It's best to be good
At one with God
The devil should turn
His back from you
And all the others
For you follow the path
Of God and you
So sort of know it
A church is there
For those who want
To be at one with God
Much has to be
Rewrote in this age
Of those who have
Closed minds closed souls
Who never see the light
Who never know of
The soul and what
It means to those
So very religious so
Embraced in things holy
God wants the world
To live to the old
Holy Bible scriptures so
Read them and know

Richard Clewlow

MY SECRET GARDEN

In my mind, there is a garden.
A lovely resting place.
I come to visit often
When I need a little space.
It brings to me a peace of mind
I close my eyes and dream
If I listen close enough
I even hear the stream.
It flows so gently beneath the trees
It ripples onward,
Bringing calm to please,
Abundant perfumes fragrance the air
Blossoms crown tree tops
Their beauty quite rare.
Flower beds blazing with wondrous colour
They freely give their pleasure.
A wonderful feeling
Forever to treasure.
I sit in my garden
And savour the calm
Free from all heartache
And safe from all harm.
Oh how I love to linger here.
I see my loved one's smile.
Thank You Lord for giving me.
This garden for a while.

Rita Dilks

THE MIRROR

You call me into being.
Reflecting
I nothing am
and all things are not
without you
and you
and you
both dead and living.

I pray
God
come
call my being closer
through you
and you
and you
both dead and living.

That seeing
I nothing am
and all things are
nothing but reflection
your mirror
may begin to register
nothing but light from your heaven.

Judith Garrett

A HELPING HAND

Climb up over boulders
Rise towards the sun
At the dawning of a new day
And living just begun
Rise up o'er rocks and trials
Strewn along life's way
With your hand in God's Hand
To help you thro' each day.

Mary Hayworth

WITH GOD ALL IS POSSIBLE

I take a step and stumble.
Bruised and scratched I carry on
Thinking as I go, God is there,
With God all is possible.

To fall often is our human lot.
To receive knocks and scrapes
And be soothed with God's balm
Is the reason we carry on along life's path.

God is everywhere, full of possibility.
Seeing all, knowing all, hearing all.
All He asks is our love, our trust, our faith
And in return He is Our Father.

I take a step and stumble.
Bruised and scratched I carry on
Thinking as I go, God is there,
With God all is possible.

Gabrielle Hopkins

TO MY CHILD

My child, my precious child,
your bright soul danced within me
all too briefly.

My child, my precious child,
you left me empty.
Empty of all except the cry 'Why?'
Empty of you.

My child, my precious child,
you took so much.
My dreams, my hopes of all that you would do.

My child, my precious child,
you gave so much.
In your coming.
In becoming.
In your very being.
You gave me, precious child,
the precious gift of parenthood.

My child, my precious child,
you taught so much.
That love is not confined in flesh.
Nor chained to time.
Nor crushed by death.

My child, my precious child,
your bright soul dances still.
In the heart of creation.
In the freedom of eternity.
Within the arms of God.

Marion Adams

GIVING

Love the sun, for it shines its warmth upon you,
Love the moon because it lights the darkest hours.
Love the world because it loves you too.
Love the soil for all the beauty of its flowers.
Love the trees for sweeping clean the air,
Their green leaves bringing welcome shade.
Love the rain that helps to keep them there,
Love the quietness of the sheltered glade.
Let your eyes rest upon nature's beauty.
See the animals that God made,
Respect and love all things that live,
Help wherever help is needed.
And if you have spare love to give,
When you've tried to give so much.
Give a little love to me,
I who love you much too much.

Marjorie Maude Walter

HAVE FAITH

Have faith in the Lord and the
          world will become
A much safer place for everyone
there will be no more cheating
          and no more lying
No more stealing and no more spying

The cheating will stop and people will be
          cheerful and happy and forever free
there will be no more murders
          and no more drugs
just a big happy world
if you believe in the Lord above.

I Blair

PRAYER

Heal me, angels up above.
Let me cope with life when rough.
Allow me to help others bring,
the life force they have within.

Let my inner feelings glow
and my instincts to know
when I'm doing all right
not let others forever gripe.

I have no option, I will use
the force within me, I'll not lose.
Be there, help me find my goal,
let the light guide my soul.

So when I'm low and lost the sight,
don't let go, when I'm in plight.
Show me how to lift my thoughts,
so I'm no longer out of sorts.

To love others and be loved too,
is a gift that all should woo.
Cherish all moments, good or bad,
they'll help you, so don't be sad.

Negative thoughts are banished from,
your mind and thoughts, forever gone.
Positive thoughts are now king
and in my soul will ever sing.

Gena Crawford

TAKE MY HAND

My child this is a cruel world,
A world of hurt and pain,
Of broken trust and shattered dreams,
Of sin and wrong to all mankind,
        Take my hand.

The past is very frightening,
The future is too hard to face,
There is nowhere to flee,
But to this present place in time.
        Please, take my hand.

I cannot take away, the hurts that you have felt,
I cannot make your memories fade,
But I can be with you,
As you recall your hurt and pain.
Just take my hand.

Feel my touch and feel my warmth,
Feel the clasp of my embrace,
Words are not needed,
For I am here.
Hold my hand.

It says, I am with you,
I care about you deeply,
I want to be there for you,
Can't you see I understand?

I too have felt your hurt and pain,
Your agony and tears,
But as you walk life's pathway,
I will walk with you as you with me -
        Feel my hand in yours!

Yvonne Smyth

AS YOU CHOOSE!

I gazed at the picture of Jesus
I thought with mild surprise,
He can't be God. He doesn't smile
Then I looked into His eyes.

Those piercing eyes, I looked again
His arms were stretched out wide
I caught a glimpse of Calvary
His precious blood, a crimson tide.

He was waiting there for me
To run into His arms and hide
Accepted, forgiven, safe from harm
Held close to His wounded side.

Forgive me Lord for all my sins
Was laid on You that day
You washed me in Your precious blood
Cleansing me. Showing me 'the way'.

Thank You for making me
A daughter of the King
For dying for me, for choosing me
Accept the praise I bring,

Please show me how to serve You Lord,
May others see my love for You
In every aspect of my life
In everything I say and do.

I stood before the picture of Jesus
I gazed at His dear, dear face
'Till He come' my spirit cries
See in His eyes such love, such grace.

Alice Carlin

MY HIDING PLACE

Oh Lord I'm weary of this life
The pain, the anguish, tears and strife
The days are hard, the nights so long
Laughter seems forgotten, pleasures gone
It's very hard to focus on
The joys that have gone before
Father in your grace and mercy
Let those times come once more
Lord help me to remember
The blessing you have bestowed
The Rock that I can cling too
When I feel 'at the end of the road'
Thank you loving Father for your tender care.
The feeling of belonging when no-one else is there.
You are my strength, my hiding place.
Fill me Father with your loving grace.

Barbara Symons

TESTIMONY

The mind is quiet now,
the strain of recent years is past;
the anxious brow no longer so.
The thoughts which seemed to find no peace
are still at last with those which come from God,
strong in His strength.
The heart which had no rest found calm at length
where Home is for the soul as Haven for the boat at sea;
respite for the weary; remission of an agony;
where righteousness and mercy meet and,
journeying on with eager feet,
the pilgrim hears 'Just hold my hand'.

C Ochiltree

THE BIBLE!

Some say the bible is just a book
then if that's what you think
just take a look
it teaches about wisdom
love, peace and joy
teaches about compassion
and a baby boy
A boy that grows up into a man
Man with a purpose and a plan
A plan and a purpose for you and me
to do and say and be
What we are meant to be
To be loved by God and live His way
and let Him help us each and every day
Jesus came to set us free
After all isn't that what we all long to be
Totally and 100% born again
   Free!

L A Clark

SURRENDER

From what are you hiding?
Why this anger and hate?
Why this facade? It's never too late
To face the hurt, to face the pain,
Offer it to God, again and again.
Trust in His love and welcome His care.
Surrender your spirit, lay your soul bare.
A Peace will follow, enveloping, embracing,
To sustain you forever, what e'er you are facing.

Elizabeth Ness

TAKE THE TIME

Take the time to see God's beauty
That surrounds us everywhere.
Mountains, valleys, rivers flowing
Nothing can with these compare

In the garden flowers appearing
soon they grow and in full bloom,
all the colours of the rainbow
fills the air with sweet perfume

Fields of corn spread like a blanket
growing strong beneath the sun.
getting ready for the harvest
with willing hands the work is done

See the trees so tall and slender
Hear the wind its whispering sound.
autumn leaves are gently falling
Watch them floating to the ground

Snow and ice has its own beauty
as the flakes come fluttering down,
children laughing building snowmen
Happy faces no time to frown

We thank you Lord you took the time
to give us all these pleasures.
if only we would realise
You are our greatest treasure.

R Smith

A GRAIN OF SAND

To see a world in a grain of sand,
The poet dreams and why not more?
For in those grains of sand,
A universe might stand;
And in those worlds therein,
Intelligence, for sure.

Again, in universes vast,
Other worlds may be,
In numbers unbelievable,
For thus the mould is cast,
Within those unseen worlds,
A multiplicity, eternity.

Our universe that we now see,
This world of ours, our land,
Our seas and all within,
Sets in the mind a query,
For if the poet's dream is true,
What around our sand, has God so mercifully planned?

Iolo Lewis

THAT'S LIFE

To see your child for the very first time
To know that your love will always be mine.
To be tucked up in bed, all cosy and warm
To see a blue sky at the end of a storm.
That's life.

To smell the perfume, from a flower in bloom
To hope that all wars will end very soon
To hold a small bird, in the palm of your hand
To sit on a beach with your feet in the sand
That's life.

To cry when things aren't going so well
To laugh and be happy, with good news that you tell
To look at the stars, as they shimmer and shine
To join in with singing at Christmas time.
That's life.

To believe in the Father, Son and Holy Ghost
To help everyone, and not count the cost.
To see the sunset, at the end of the day
To worship your God, in your own special way
That's life . . .

Gig

A BEAUTIFUL TRUTH

I used to be weary and sad at heart;
Walking blindly through the days;
Having no goal or reason to achieve;
A soul walking the wrong way.

Then one day; the greatest day
That I'll never forget,
I found a truth so beautiful,
So honest and yet
It laid down no special laws;
No promise of pain for my sin,
But a gentle persuading truth
That invited goodness in.

And into my heart that truth brought
So much peace on me to rest;
A soul having found itself'
But here is the best;
I know now that when I die
I need not be filled with dread,
But only to fear death as much
As I fear going to bed.

Mavis Hardy

LOVE

I have given my life for love,
and in the perfect form above,

For life may be the darkest storm,
but in that darkness love is born,

A love of thought, a love of hope,
a way to see, a way to cope,

I look to God, He will be my way,
and pray for strength, His love will say.

John Daw

UNTITLED

So many people in this world strive,
Not knowing Jesus Christ is alive.
In how many homes lies the Holy book.
Where no-one bothers to take a look.
Left on a shelf gathering dust,
Words of God's goodness, love and trust.
Pages full of such wonderful tales,
Of his compassion, mercy that never fails.
The works of God, hope of salvation,
Handed down from generation to generation.
They tell of how Jesus came to redeem us.
How God raised his son to make us righteous.
After he died on the cross, our debt to pay.
How his blood brings life, the truth, the way.
Don't believe me, take the book off the shelf,
Make sure what I say is true, read for yourself.
Don't live in ignorance learn how to be free,
How to gain life thr' Jesus for eternity.

Joyce Screeton

FREEDOM

A tranquil moment undisturbed.
To escape from reality, life's struggles to depart.
Everyone requires freedom. A place fond to their heart.
Is yours to a cornfield of golden yellow?
Swaying in the breeze from the wind's blow.
Or a burbly swishing river flowing with trout.
Watched a spreading ripple where a fish leapt out.
Alleviated the sound of crashing waves of the sea.
That's my comforting sound my solace to me.
Eluded waters under a concrete bridge
Churning below, beneath and between rocky ridge.
Across to the mystical beauty of the Isle of Skye.
To rich red cullins, mountain rising high.
That's my comforting sight my pulchritude to me.
Do you like to walk in a pine forest after a storm?
To engulf the smell of nature's fresh charm
Prefer I. Alone to watch the pink sunset hue.
Or espy a spider's web, wet with early morning dew.
    That's my tranquil moment.
      My peaceful freedom to me.

Yvonne Fraser

THE CONVENT

I wandered round the cloisters within those ancient walls.
My thoughts went back to long ago; I fancied I heard calls.
So many feet have traversed along that well-worn path;
So many have found comfort and peace of mind at last.

So many problems solved at length after much serious thought,
By prayer and meditation and things that can't be bought.
A wander round the cloisters where all is quiet and still,
Makes one to feel so humble and try to do God's will.

A E Kendall

FLOWERS

Catkins in spring and pussy willow,
Snowdrops, violets and crocus below.
Later a wonderful carpet of bluebells
Whilst cowslip and primrose peep in the dells.
Down in the ditch the celandine grows.
What soft yellow light the daffodil throws.

Wild in the summer the daisy and buttercup,
Forget-me-not, foxglove and yellow kingcup.
Out in the green field the sweetened pink clover,
Out in the corn field the soft blue cornflower.
Wild in the summer wherever you look:
Harebell, yarrow, knapweed and yellow-orange bird's foot.

What a wonderful place the garden is to me
With tulip, narcissus, pansy, sweet pea.
There in the corner with majestic pose
The iris and fuschia, and princess: the rose.
Marigold and jasmine, perfumed wall flower,
Candytuft, honeysuckle, scented lavender.

Lining the flower bed: orange nasturtium,
Lilly of the valley, snap dragon, geranium.
In every direction a wonderful hue
Mixed with the sunlight and soft hazy blue.
But there is just one flower so special to me:
The queen of them all - the blood red poppy.

Nicky Cooper

HIDDEN TREASURE DOWN UNDER

In wilderness Down Under where water lilies bloom
Where crocodiles in still waters and birds with coloured plume
All live in scenic beauty underneath the scorching sun
But shaded by the canopy until the day is done
Where bush tucker is a delicacy and natives walk along the shore
To forage for the nice fat grubs and gladly eat them raw
Few white men see your beauty rare and creatures crouching still
For patience is what's needed to really take your fill
Galahs crowd at the water hole and suck up waters clear
But movement in the water and they quickly rise in fear
Landing now in tree tops high, they make a pink display
Like blossoms in their fullest bloom, on a bright spring day
But their squawking's not like flowers and the screeching fills the air
As again they land on shoreline and fight to get their share
A wallaby now shows himself and drinks in waters sweet
Some dingo pups have been here too, for the mud reveals their feet
Bright dragon fly buzz in the air to land on lilypads green
And scores of water birds taking flight create a splashing scene
What hidden beauty is this sight and how it brings much pleasure
Oh how I love the wilderness, oh what a hidden treasure
God has made the wilderness, and has brought us to this day
He also created you and me, let's come to Him and pray
Let's praise Him for his goodness and all His mighty power
And let us know that 'He is God' even in this hour.

Marlene Peckham

IF YOU WOULD ONLY PRAY

We are praying for you
although I have never met
you; that doesn't matter.
The fact is we care enough
to pray for you.

We are praying for you, for
God hears our prayers and
sees your loneliness

We are praying for you, and
asking for God to help with
all your difficulties in your
home.

We are praying for you, do
you live on your own
Then take heart for you will
never be on your own, for
doesn't God live with you.

We are praying for you, for
being aware of our Christian
duty,
We are only too willing to
offer prayers for the needy
of our community

We are praying for you, have
you got a problem or two
and it won't go away.
I am sure you will find a
solution if you would only
pray.

E Rehill

THE REVIVAL

Do you want revival,
Are you prepared to start,
With a supply of living water,
And *Jesus* in your heart.

Do you feel you have no power,
And nothing you can give,
Just call upon your 'Saviour'
For help your life to live.

He, said you only need to ask,
To seek and you will find,
Knock and it will be opened up to you,
But leave old ways behind.

The sins that lie within you,
Just lay at *Jesus* feet,
He has promised *He* will bear them,
And our daily wants to meet.

Now draw a circle round you,
Then in it kneel and pray,
That when you step outside it,
You'll be ready for the fray.

So as your will grows stronger,
And your Faith in *Him* is true,
That *Revival* will be started,
And *He* has chosen you.

Do not take this task too lightly,
There is much that must be done,
But with *Christ's* help you can do it,
And the wayward soul be won.

Will A Tilyard

THIS IS THE END
(Written in hospital after my stroke, 1993)

Thio io the ond
For all I ever was
Upon this earth . . .
This antithesis of birth

I've run the race
Contributed my bit
In this short life
This is the end to all the strife

That I have known
And as I go to rest
My weary bones
Will soon be resting under stones

That have been around
More years than human life
Yet still persist
And will long after we exist.

Thank goodness it wasn't the end!

Maxwell Bruce

MY BEST TO YOU

May you be blest with life's true love
So you live in a happy home
May you be there for one another
So you never walk alone

May troubles never tarry long
Soon disappear from view
And if dark clouds loom up high
May there be a splash of blue

May whatever your plans may be
May they be right for you
Peaceful times fill your days
And friends prove to be true

May joy be where so ere you tread
So in time to come you'll find
A trail of laughter's footprints
On the road you left behind.

Adela Llewellyn

A POET'S DREAM

They call it a poet's dream, to find the words of love,
to say great things of feelings, some of us may know,
words elude the wise, and make him really wonder why,
a love can just take over, and change his way of life.

Many others will agree, it's where they want to be,
there with someone special, making poetry,
to see Heaven here right now, sure of every move,
and never need to search again, around for something new.

If I became that poet, I'd know just what to say,
I'd mention every detail, of how I feel today,
I'd say that all the world should know, how to love again,
how to reach each other, and call a stranger friend.

I'd say that in the heart of us, there's a poem that must be read,
there's a love that wants to surface, there's words that must be said,
if only in a whisper, with meaning they belong,
to bring sweet lines of comfort, to reassure each one.

They call it a poet's dream, to find the words of love,
to understand creation, each leaf and opening bud,
to sweep the colours of a rainbow, across a darkened sky,
and lift the heart of earthling man, and let life's poem rhyme.

M Bell

INFORMATION

We hope you have enjoyed reading this book - and that you will continue to enjoy it in the coming years.

If you like reading and writing poetry drop us a line, or give us a call, and we'll send you a free information pack.

Write to

Triumph House Information
1-2 Wainman Road
Woodston
Peterborough
PE2 7BU